# In the Museum of My Daughter's Mind

# In the Museum of My Daughter's Mind

poems by

Marjorie Maddox

featuring art by

Anna Lee Hafer

Contributing Artists: Karen Elias, Antar Mikosz, Greg Mort,
Margaret Munz-Losch, Ingo Swann, and Christian Twamley

SHANTI ARTS PUBLISHING

BRUNSWICK, MAINE

**In the Museum of My Daughter's Mind**



Published by Shanti Arts Publishing
Designed by Shanti Arts Designs

Cover image by Anna Lee Hafer and used with her permission

Artists who have contributed to this book and whose work has been used with their permission are Karen Elias, Anna Lee Hafer, Antar Mikosz (permission conveyed by Amerian Visionary Art Museum), Greg Mort, Margaret Munz-Losch, Ingo Swann (permission conveyed by niece Elly Flippen), and Christian Twamley.

Shanti Arts LLC
193 Hillside Road
Brunswick, Maine 04011

shantiarts.com

Printed in the United States of America

ISBN: 978-1-956056-74-7 (softcover)

Library of Congress Control Number: 2023930454

*For all the artists who teach us to see,*
*but especially for my daughter,*
*who every day bestows new sight and insight*

# Contents

# Acknowledgments

*About Place Journal:* "At the American Visionary Art Museum: *Return to the Moon*" (poem), *Return to the Moon* (painting)

*Ars Medica:* "At the American Visionary Art Museum: *The Gateway*" (poem), *The Gateway* (painting)

*Chautauqua:* "At the American Visionary Art Museum: *The Watcher*" (poem)

*The Curator:* "At the American Visionary Art Museum: *Black Cat*" (poem), *Black Cat* (painting)

*The Ekphrastic Review:* "Ark" (poem), *Ark* (mixed media); "At the American Visionary Art Museum: *Highways*" (poem); "At the American Visionary Art Museum: *Madre Dolorosa*" (poem); "The Choice" (poem), *The Library* (mixed media); "Noise" (poem), *Noise* (mixed media); "Whether with Borders" (poem), *Whether with Borders* (composite photograph)

*Ekstasis:* "Two Poems after Two Photographs by Karen Elias" (poem), *Inverted Ligularia, Ligularia in Black and White* (composite photographs)

*Glint: "Whether with Borders"* (poem), *Whether with Borders* (composite photograph); "Your Move?" (poem), *Your Move* (mixed media)

*Innisfree Poetry Journal:* "Inarticulate Archive" (poem), *Inarticulate Archive* (mixed media)

*The Inflectionist Review:* "Swirl" (poem), *Swirl* (mixed media)

*IthacaLit:* "At the American Visionary Art Museum: *Peepish Poe*" (poem), *Peepish Poe* (installation)

*The MacGuffin:* "Ante Meridiem/Post Meridiem" (poem) with a QR code to mixed media of the same names; "At the American Visionary Art Museum: *Villa's Universe*" (poem), *Villa's Universe* (painting)

*Mezzo Cammin,* "Still Life of House Plant and Trash Can" (poem)

*Open: A Journal of Arts & Letters* (and broadsides): "At the American Visionary Art Museum: *Black Cat*" (poem), *Black Cat* (painting); "At the American Visionary Art Museum: *White Rabbit*" (poem), *White Rabbit* (painting); "High Top" (poem), *High Top* (mixed media); "Metaphysical Vault" (poem), *Metaphysical Vault* (mixed media); "Switch" (poem), *Switch* (mixed media); "X-ray" (poem), *Chiaroscuro* (composite photograph)

*The Penn Review:* "The Letter E" (poem), *The Letter E* (mixed media)

*The Pine Cone Review:* "King Street" (poem), *King Street* (mixed media); "Transcendental Interstate" (poem), *Transcendental Interstate* (mixed media)

*Schuylkill Valley Journal:* "Sun on South Street" (poem)

*Sheila-Na-Gig* online: "Bare Minimum" (poem), *Bare Minimum* (mixed media)

*Southern Florida Poetry Review:* "Remnants of Marjorie Maddox"

*Still Point Arts Quarterly:* "Illegitimately Trained" (poem), *Illegitimately Trained* (mixed media); *Inarticulate Archive* (mixed media); *The Letter E* (mixed media); *The Library* (mixed media); *Metaphysical Vault* (mixed media); *Swirl* (mixed media)

*The Westchester Review:* "Naming Creation" (poem), *Swarm* (mixed media)

---

In addition, the author is most grateful to the following artists, in order of appearance, for the use of their exceptional work: Anna Lee Hafer, Margaret Munz-Losch, Ingo Swann (used by permission of the artist's niece Elly Flippen), Karen Elias, Greg Mort, and Christian Twamley.

Additional thanks are due to Founder and Director Rebecca Alban Hoffberger and to Registrars Diana Van Wagner and Connor Dorbin at the American Visionary Art Museum in Baltimore for providing images—including permission to use a photograph of *The Gateway* by Antar Mikosz—and for strong support of this project. I also would like to thank Julie L. Moore, Nicole Miyashiro, and Robbi Nester for their helpful suggestions, and publisher extraordinaire Christine Cote for her great enthusiasm for, skill with, and dedication to creating such beautiful books. Finally, my gratitude to my husband, Gary R. Hafer, for his steadfast support of both poet wife and artist daughter.

## Entering the Gallery

In May of 2018, I drove three hours with my daughter, then an undergraduate art student, to the American Visionary Art Museum in Baltimore. Or rather, I should say, my daughter, Anna Lee Hafer, drove me, her hands tightly clenching the wheel as she fearlessly navigated the expressway through a blinding thunderstorm. The week before, I had undergone an exhausting heart catheterization after an abnormal stress test. Haunted by my father's heart disease and premature death twenty-five years prior, I was looking to escape my fears. I also was looking to spend time with a daughter who had battled her own close calls.

Why did we visit this museum, one unknown to us despite numerous previous trips to Baltimore? I had seen a social media posting for AVAM's *The Great Mystery Show Exhibition*, which included Margaret Munz-Losch's two tender but unsettling portraits of her daughter. In one painting, the child's skin squirms with maggots; in another, her skin buzzes with bees. Drawn to the tension between the deceptively innocent and the dangerous, I immediately sent the exhibition information to my daughter. Yes, we agreed; we needed to go.

And just like that, one artistic expression opened into another and then another and another. That day's rainy excursion and the engaging works we encountered underscored our intersecting passions of art and poetry. It also, I now believe, spoke to us—as art does—about our separate and shared experiences, both joyous and traumatic.

In the year that followed, my daughter would complete her art degree and celebrate her first exhibit and professional sale. I would compose a series of nine poems (included in this book) based on the AVAM exhibit, art that spoke to me deeply and powerfully, caused me to gasp in wonder, and in some cases prompted me to laugh out loud. Later, those ekphrastic responses would fuel my collaboration with photographer Karen Elias on our book *Heart Speaks, Is Spoken For* (Shanti Arts, 2022). Four new collaborations with Karen are included here. Both ekphrastic series intersected with another poem based on a sculptural installation that, by mere coincidence years earlier, employed my name.

Ekphrasis is a way for art and poem, artist and poet, and writer and reader to communicate. On a personal level, I found it also deepened communication—artist to artist, mother to daughter— through an exchange of eighteen pieces based on Anna Lee's work. Those interactions constitute the core of this collection. The relationship of words and images in each poem respond to the interweaving of images and words in each painting. In composing these works, I was especially intrigued by the various ways words, numbers, and arrows become central to the paintings' overall themes. Often, I incorporated the phrases I found within a painting or artist's statement (indicated by italics) within each ekphrasis. For example, you'll find snippets of the artist's statement for *The Library* in the poem "The Choice." Likewise, in both the painting *Swirl* and the accompanying poem, you may recognize excerpts from a medication's list of possible side effects. Also, the poems "Your Move?" and "Inarticulate Archive" employ phrases woven throughout their respective paintings. Sometimes, such tight integrations resonate through the form of pantoum, sestina, villanelle, or mirror cinquain. As is often the case with artistic expression, what appears between the lines or brush strokes echoes, underscores, or comments upon the work as a whole.

This afternoon as I am writing in front of our family room's fireplace, the season's first ice storm has moved out of the area. My artist daughter is driving—not through a torrential spring downpour, but on a cold, sunny day—back to her own home a hundred miles away. Before leaving, however, she has hung her painting *The Library*, a Christmas present from my husband, above the room's "reading" chair.

To view this room in art's many rooms, I need only turn my head. And you, dear reader, need only to turn the pages.

Marjorie Maddox<br>Williamsport, Pennsylvania<br>December 2022

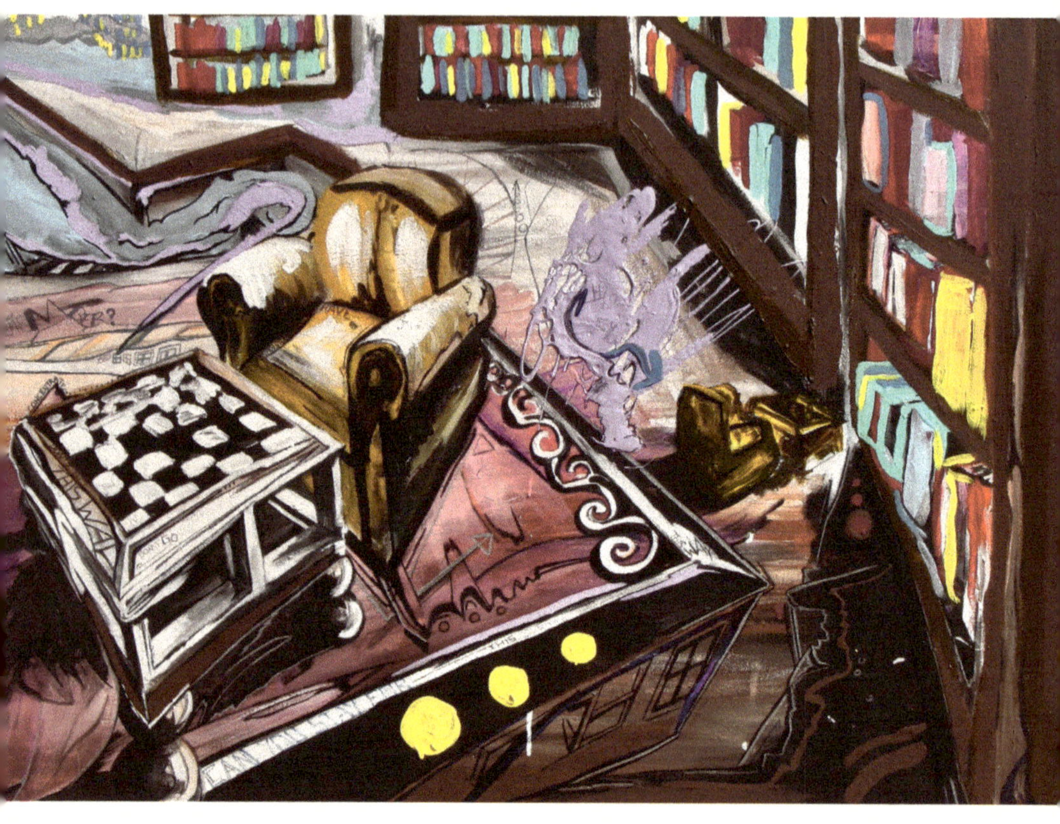

Anna Lee Hafer, *The Library*, 2019

This painting represents the inner workings of the mind. Each decision directly affects another. What move in chess shall we open with? What book shall we pull from the shelves? What path shall we take today through this library?

## The Choice

—after the painting *The Library* by Anna Lee Hafer

Late night, mid-morning, dawn,
the door of the library clicks open,
cracks wide to rooms of elsewhere
& beyond—imagination's Open-Sésame

to other doors, libraries, landscapes. Click open
possibility. *What book shall we pull from the shelves?*
Beyond Open-Sésames, imagination's magic
enters the mind's inner workings, gathers

possibilities. *What book shall we pull from the shelves?*
What ancient treasure tug from the tale?
The mind's inner workings enter in, gather
tools of chessboard and floor, bookcase stacked

with tale and treasure, the ancient why
of creation sparking each synapse
of stacked choice: chess, ceiling, floor, books—tools
to chisel word and image onto the shaped space

of creation. Sparking each synapse,
the mind reaches beyond reason to memory,
chisels word and image onto the shaped spaces
of now, before, maybe, if—choice

the reason the mind reaches beyond memory,
mirroring the large and small. *This way.*
Choose now, before, maybe, if—
or not. *Your turn. Concentrate.*

Mirror the large and small. *This way.*
*Do you remember? Can you stay?*
*Yes? No? Your turn. Concentrate.*
*What move in chess shall we open with?*

*Do you remember? Can you stay?*
What voice is woven in the fabric?
*What move in chess shall we open with?*
Follow the arrows to pawn or king.

What voice is woven in the fabric?
Here is the story of Open-Sésame.
Follow the arrows to pawn or king,
rooftop or floorboards. *Don't go*

without a story. Open-Sésame
your way to elsewhere & beyond.
Climb rooftops. Sketch floorboards. Go.
*What path shall we take today through this library?*

This way to elsewhere & beyond.
A splatter is not a mistake, but a choice.
*What path shall we take today through this library?*
Follow the inner workings of the mind.

A splatter is a choice, not a mistake.
Cracks open the room to elsewhere.
Always the inner workings of the mind follow
choice. Each dawn, mid-morning, night,

crack open rooms to elsewhere.
You hold the pen and paintbrush.
Late-night, mid-morning, or dawn, choose
imagination. Click open the door to the library.

---

*Italicized phrases are taken from the artist's description of the work, as well as from words and phrases hidden within the painting. For a closeup of the work, go to www.hafer.work.

## Naming Creation

—after the painting *Swarm* by Anna Lee Hafer

From her mouth

letters transform *swarm*. Her pursed lips
release a kiss of them, explosion of light
and swirl that redefines the way words slip

from cortex to cochlea. Their circular dip
into dance and sense twirls at dusk, border of night/
day transformed in the swarm. Her letters purse lips,

beget articulation—reverse total eclipse
until inspiration's bright flash of lights
swirls, redefines the way words slip,

spark synapse after synapse after synapse
while hand, brain, memory, insight
transform the letters to *warms*. Her pursed lips

release painting & poem. No planned script
can recreate such abundance of bright
swirl that defines the way words slip

into meaning, transmission of firefly blips
igniting the mind's sky with inspiration. To write
letters transformed by swarming, purse lips

and swirl vision. Like this, redefined words slip

from her mouth

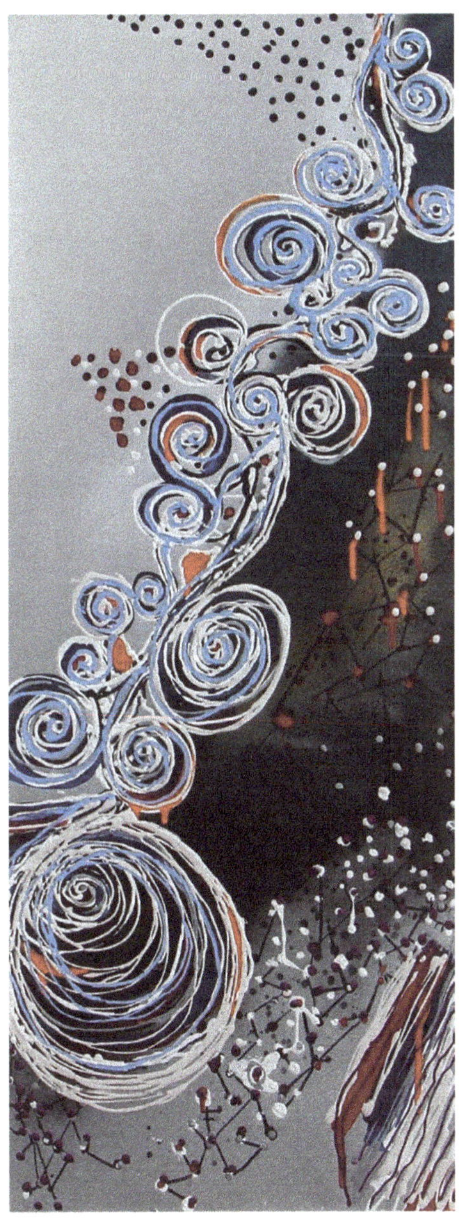

Anna Lee Hafer,
*Swarm*, 2021

The word *swarm* has such negative connotations. The first hits on the internet reference a swarm of 55 earthquakes striking off the Oregon Coast and a step-by-step guide on how to rid your area from swarms of insects. However, what happens when the word *swarm* is viewed in a more positive light?

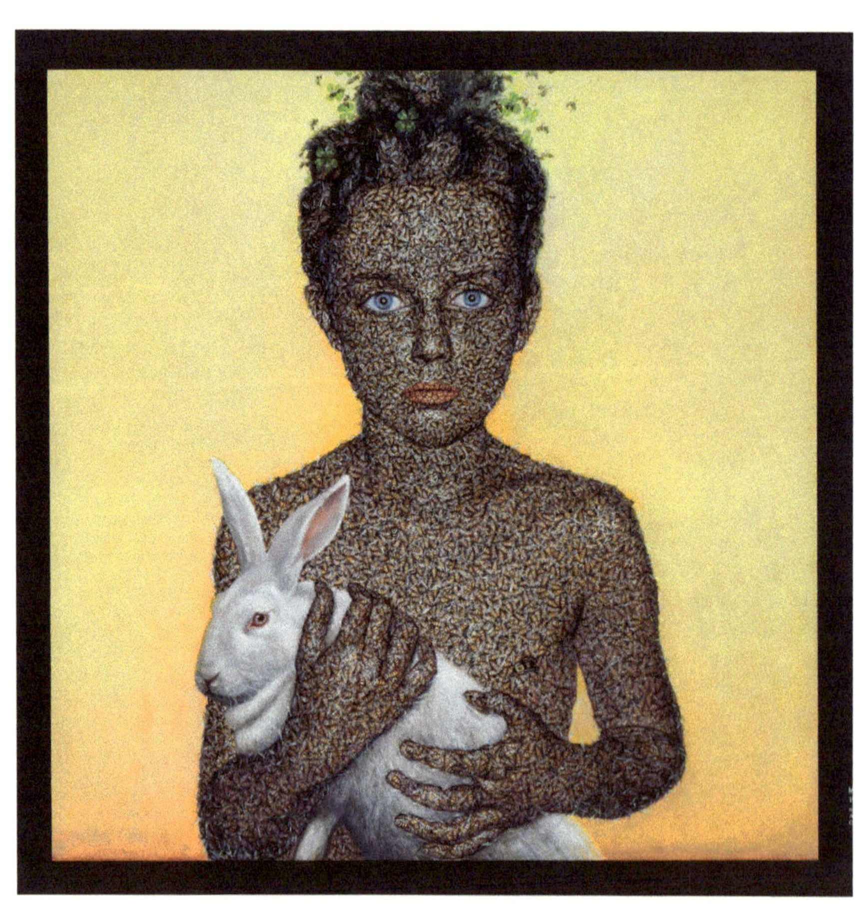

Margaret Munz-Losch, *White Rabbit*, 2008

## At the American Visionary Art Museum: *White Rabbit*

—from *Beauty and the Beast* by Margaret Munz-Losch

Eyes the pale blue-
gray of cornflowers,
the naked girl buzzes
with bees, is bees: nipple,
elbows, neck, chest, swarming
forehead; insect fingers grasping
the starkly white, pink-eyed,
magician's rabbit of miracles
paired with the good-luck clovers
sprouting from her dirt-blonde bun
crawling with workaholic drones loyal
to scent and perceived innocence,
the way my mother skin
tingles with hers, is hers/
yours, tiny stings that cling
to the most vulnerable
flesh left to love, hovering
sweetly, deceptively,
over the decaying, the dead.

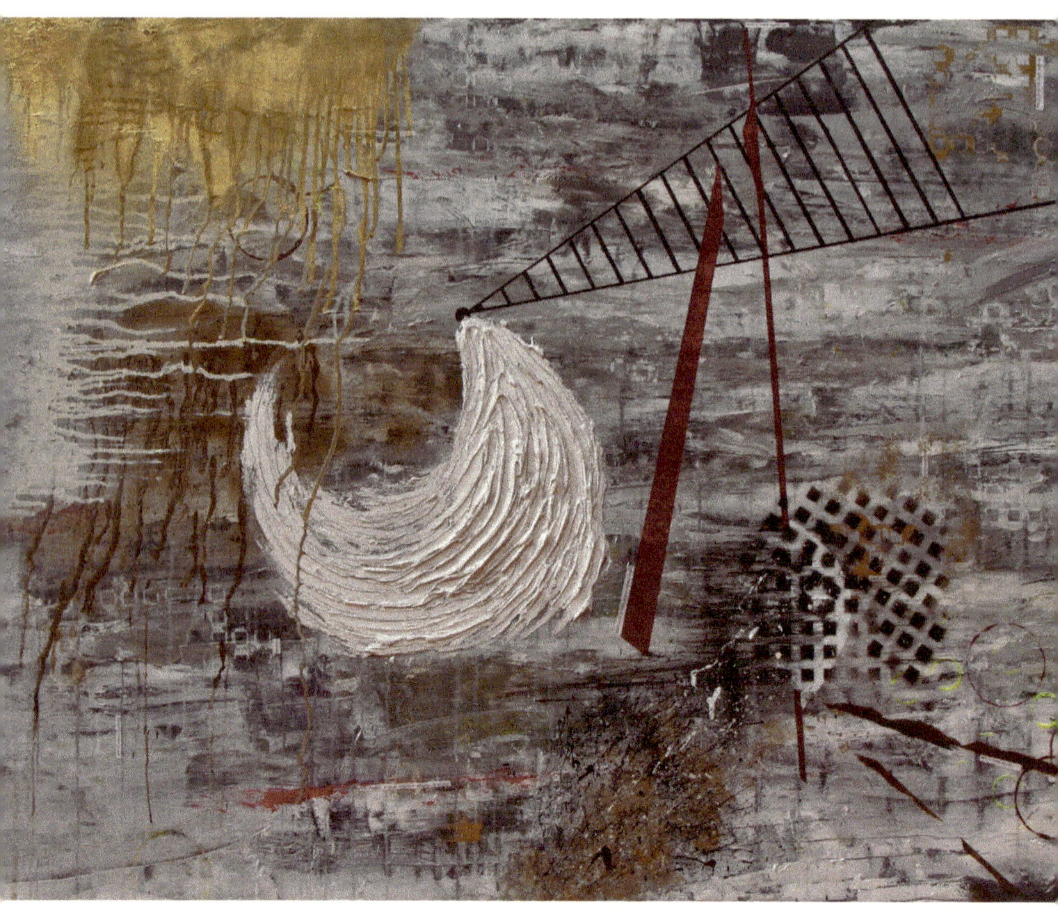

Anna Lee Hafer, *Swirl*, 2018

*Swirl* exhibits strong visual elements of harmony and balance, but with a closer look, a contradictory message occurs.

## Swirl*

—after the painting by Anna Lee Hafer

Look closer. This is not a textbook, but a person.
This is not a painting but the poem of someone's mind,
her mind: *new or worse depression.*
Beneath the surface of *harmonious balance,*

this is not a painting but the poem of someone's mind.
*Thoughts about suicide or dying*
beneath the surface of *harmonious balance.*
*New or worse irritability, new or worse anxiety,*

*thoughts about suicide or dying—*
phrases that swirl, stick in the waves of brain,
*new or worse irritability, new or worse anxiety.*
This is not a final exam, but a daughter,

phrases that swirl, stick in the waves of brain,
weeping you can drown in, almost did.
This is not a final exam. This is a daughter,
who slipped beneath the surface, but rose up

from weeping. You almost drowned in it. Did.
*Being regretful, being angry, being violent,*
she slipped beneath the surface. How to rise up
*from depression or other serious mental illness?*

*Being regretful, being angry, being violent:*
anchors tugging on limbs, words. Drowning
*from depression and other serious mental illness.*
*Trouble sleeping, paranoia, reckless behavior—*

the heaviest anchors tugging on limbs, words. Drowning,
the surface dark and far away. Where is the light?
*Trouble sleeping, paranoia, reckless behavior:*
struggling against the waves just to feel something,

the surface dark and far away. Where is the light?
*Sudden changes in mood, behaviors, thoughts, or feelings:*
Struggling against the waves just to feel something,
*acting on sudden impulses.* Where is the joy?

*Sudden changes in mood, behaviors, thoughts, or feelings:*
This is not a final exam, but a daughter
*acting on sudden impulses*. Where is the joy?
The world is aswirl with fear. *Attempts to commit suicide.*

This is not a final exam, but a daughter
and her beloved life. *Treating depression:*
The world is aswirl with fear *(attempts to commit suicide)*
beneath the surface of *harmonious balance.*

This is a life of *treating depression,* both
a painting and a poem—complicated beauty of mind
beneath the surface of *harmonious balance.*
Look closer. This is not a textbook, but a person.

---

*Italicized phrases are woven into the painting or are part of the artist's statement. Many of the phrases originated from a medication's list of side effects. For a closeup of the work, go to www.hafer.work.

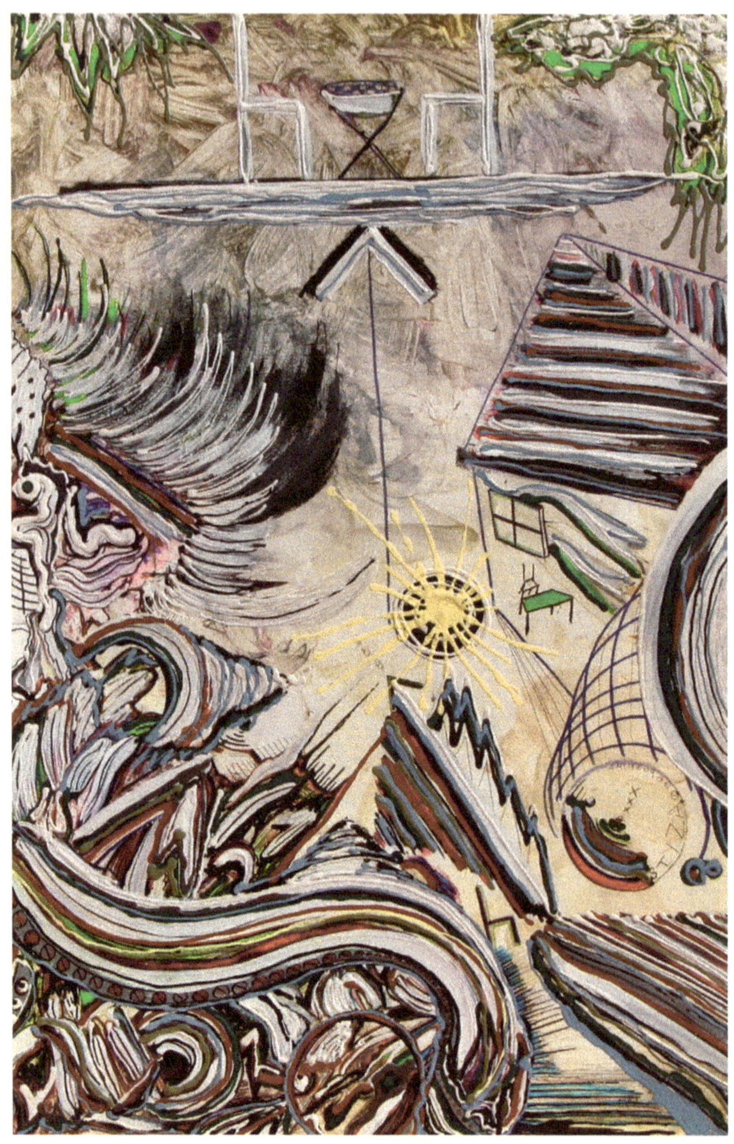

Anna Lee Hafer, *High Top*, 2021

Your own personal table with an entity? What will you discuss today? What questions do you have for the dead?

# High Top

—after the painting by Anna Lee Hafer

See-saw balance between ground
and muted sky, we ride imagination
to life, the one without vacant chairs,
chessboard absent of the pieces
we forgot to move
or bring
or pick up from the jagged noise
nine lives below
the paint-pitched roof,
the wind-swept air,
the sinking sun peering in
at other empty tables,
empty chairs.

What you are saying is
the compass-needle pole
that keeps us whole
and here,
such precarious stability
on this platform island of two
minus two.

Are we still *we*
in this unseen grief
that keeps trying
to listen to soul
and scream?

High atop the made-up,
knee-deep in nostalgia,
and miles above any
scientifically proven memories,
you initiate contact:
King's Pawn Opening.

I can almost see your breath;
you can almost touch my words—
here, high up in the beyond
waiting for the world's
next moves.

# At the American Visionary Art Museum: *The Gateway*

—artist Antar Mikosz

Even with 3D glasses, all you can see are trees
swaying in a breeze of blood beside a swampy pond
murky with nightmares. A rapist lingers somewhere
in the periphera. I, too, hear him breathing,
his damaged heart heaving inside your terror
that clings to thick vein-like trunks
patterned with geometric tastebud recipients
of bitterness—the ones in all our bloody pumps.
This is the way of perception. Fear
steers me toward the portal of your forest,
but all I can see

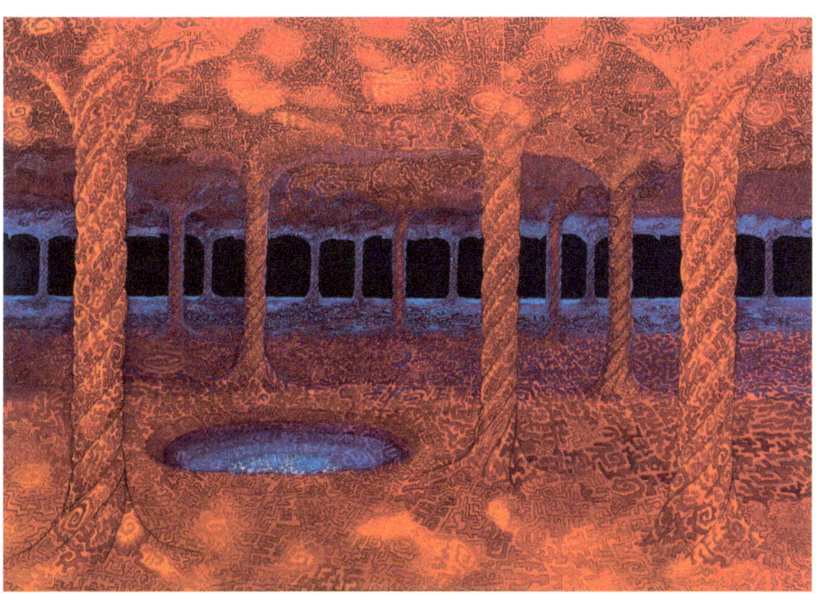

Antar Mikosz, *The Gateway*, 2013

is the inside of my father's heart,
where, from a deep hole, his donor's
car careens into scream that bubbles up
now from the pond of your words
into my father's aorta,
pulsing a rhythm of red
that remembers foggy dreams
painted by a young man
detouring an icy life into accident
or gift, this gateway mysterious
in its pathway of give and take,
in the perception of breath we can
not swallow, the visions we see
daily vibrating between
now and here, between
lovely, dark, and deep.

## Transcendental Interstate

—after the painting by Anna Lee Hafer

No monotonous monorail,
    these elevated railways

    crisscross lifelines, dip
into the infinite, traversing transcendental

possibilities that blur past at faster-
    than lightning speed

    traps. Meanwhile, you stare
out the window, round-trip-it to the sun,

firework-it to constellations, then
    I've-got-a-ticket-to-ride-it

    toward all the rails of now,
then, and in between. True, you're

a front-row witness to society's
    manic meltdown and

catastrophic collapse of
conscience. But Hey! Hey! Hey!

who's going to slow down
the intersecting trains

of thought but you?
Time to brake the spellbound

pattern of traffic, dim the neon rails
of continuous intersecting collisions.

Time to remove the gold-
colored glasses as cracked as this high-

speed chase twisting into one alternate
reality after another and

another, this inner state
of who we are—driving and driven—

speeding us all the way toward
destination's shattered end.

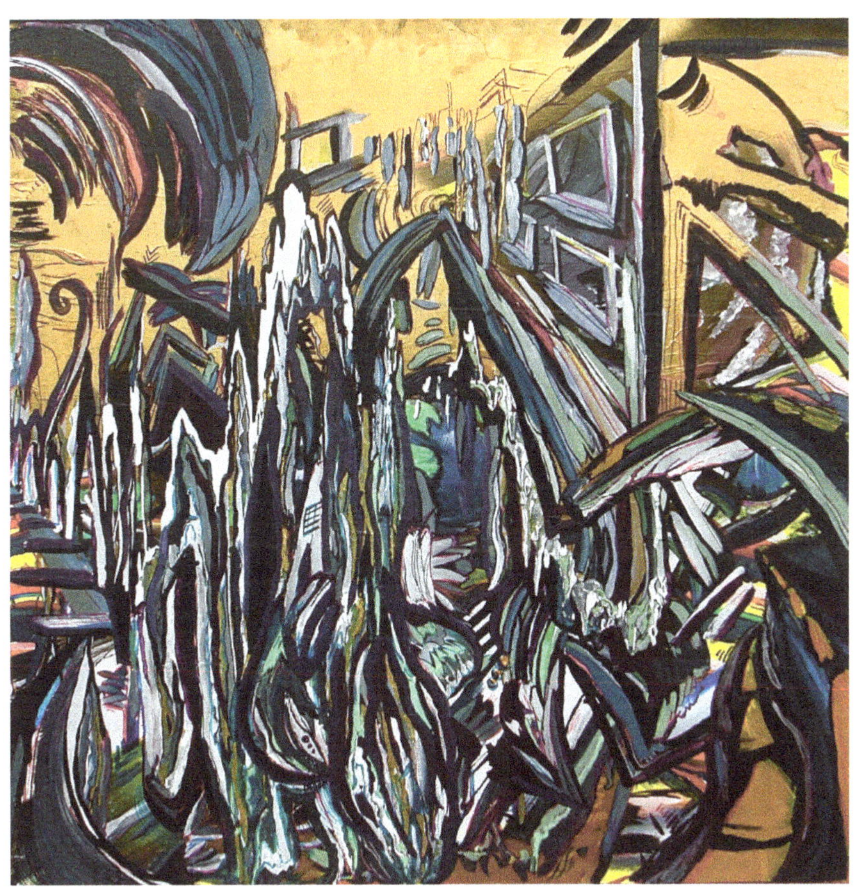

Anna Lee Hafer, *Transcendental Interstate*, 2021

In this work that travels in, through, and between infinite possible universes, we are led to a distortion of our world where buildings melt, passageways collide, and foreign forms scream at whoever is there to witness.

## At the American Visionary Art Museum: *Highways*

—artist and psychic Ingo Swann

From here he sees there,
one road running above the other,
the mystery of Mars no asphalt look-alike
but still a twin risen to enlightenment,
riding the rails of space and purple mountains majesty,
the mind's psychedelic skies just one more way
to somewhere before sailing away
to mirage from that parched desert
or uninhabitable planet
you no longer believe is
not real. Climb in.
Let's go for a spin.

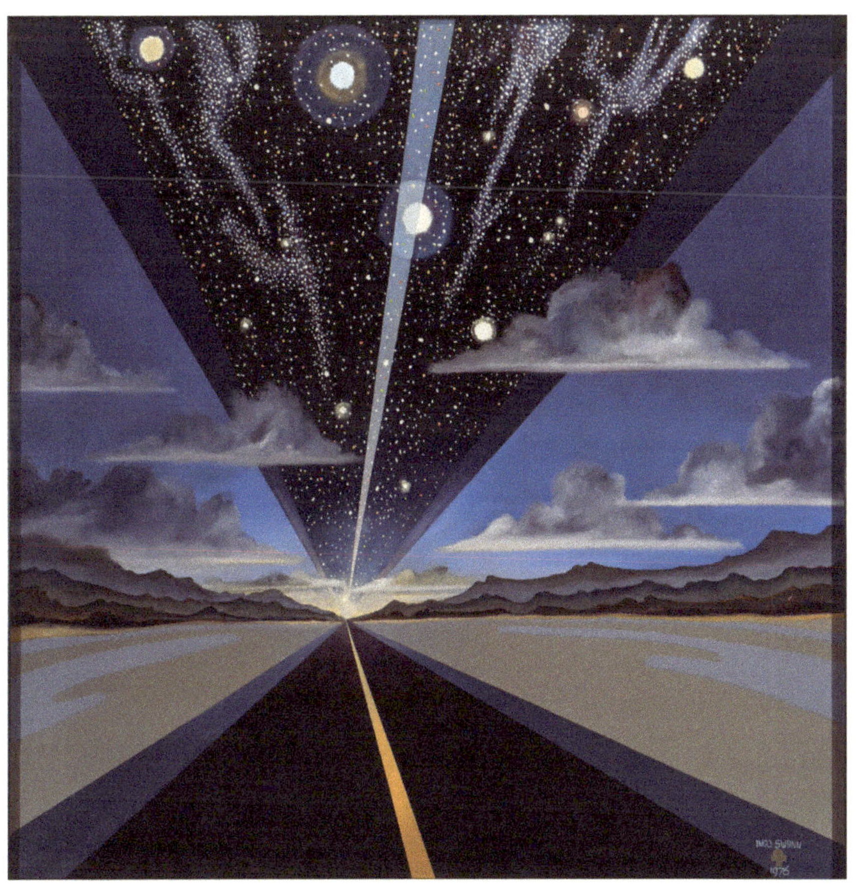


Ingo Swann, *Highways*, 1976

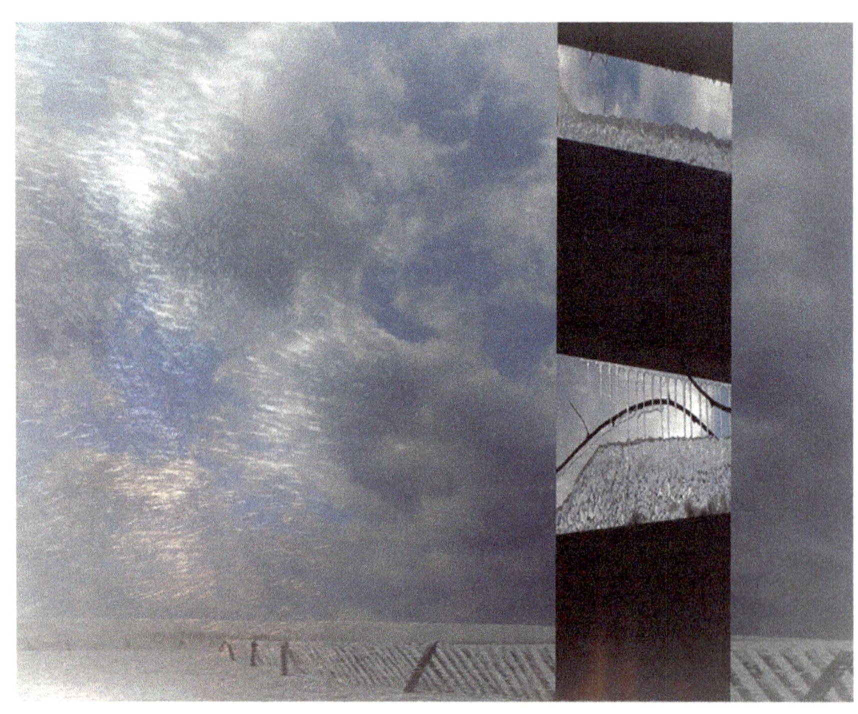

Karen Elias, *Whether with Borders*, 2013

## Whether with Borders

—after the composite photograph by Karen Elias

These seasons, you're never sure whether
the weather of *now* steps through
or over the barbed-wire borders
of others' spaces, but here the clouds—
as textured as clogged lungs—hover
precariously close to the past of *then*. Face

it; each night, you still breathe in faces
clamoring across borders—their weather
of worry: the wind that stalls and hovers
over the landscape of you. Born a nomad, you threw
shadows across lightning, watched clouds—
heavy but mute—re-form foggy borders.

Spaces, wide and open, still haunt, the sky a bad border
you can't evict. Her mottled, gray face—
begging always for mercy—keeps clouding
the view. Weather, whether, the calm eye of whatever
blur in the whirlwind you try to step through
into space that fences home, hovers

in the sun-streaked rain that hovers
with its empty promise over the bare soil. Borders
call from across the horizon. You yearn to walk to and through,
to hold close your cloak of questions and face
the unreliable temper tantrums of weather
prophesied in each Rorschach of clouds.

Fair skies/foreboding? The clichés of memory choose "cloudy,"
that fifty percent chance of happiness hovering
over your front porch seconds before you decide whether
to step off into the forecasted storm, just beyond your borders,
the ones that make you *feel* safe, but aren't. You face
the inevitable, wandering wind, then hitchhike through

any opening into the future, now through,
you promise, with all that's past. The back-lit clouds
beckon, and your aging, weathered face
forges on into the unpredictable. Hope hovers
in the breeze you breathe beyond borders
in that lush language that uncovers whether

or not each wave of weather crosses over and through
to broader spaces, gathering ancestors, former selves, all that hovers
so close now to hope, to your un-cloudy, border-less face.

# Noise

—after the painting by Anna Lee Hafer

My own

electrical storm break-
        dancing the sky of skull,

riotous riffs
        on the unpredictable.
                Even before

the EEG MC'd asymmetrical jerks,
        my tolerance for sound's
tossed out with each
                dizzying jag of note.

        Each ragged twirl,
each syncopation on steroids,
        batters the cerebral,
                cyclone gone haywire
    into some vast static of seizure.

Richter scale of cacophony—
              tornado and earthquake,
       firework and fissure—
                     ramped-up Chaos

axes the faux door,
       pummels the thin walls,
evicts balance from the brain.

       No predictable melodic
       drone sliding forward

       toward home, no Quiet
              Sweet Quiet

easing the night into calm.

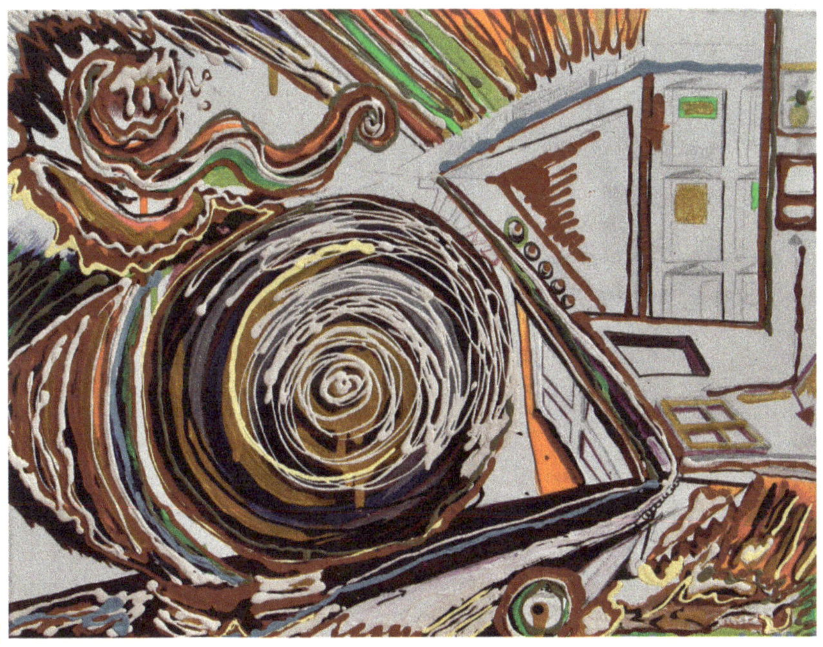

Anna Lee Hafer, *Noise*, 2021

*Noise* is a physical representation of live music performed in the city street.

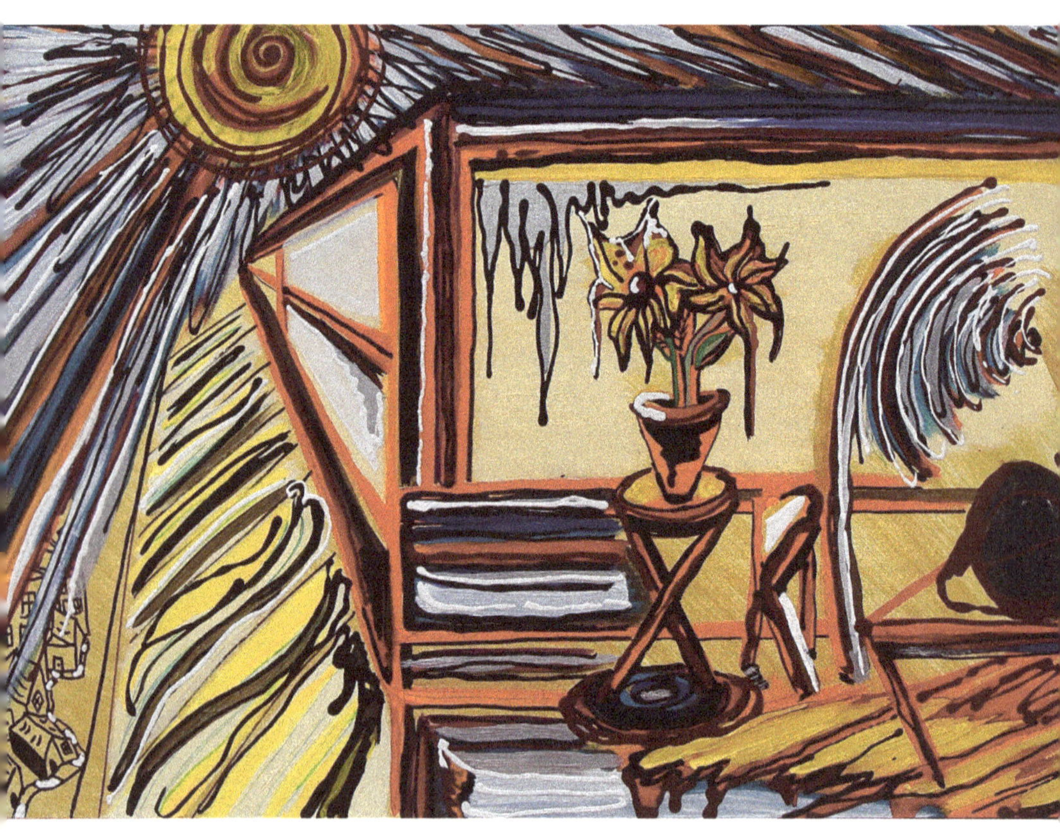

Anna Lee Hafer, *Sun on South Street*, 2019

*Sun on South Street* was inspired by the small moments of isolation found in the big, busy city.

## Sun on South Street

—after the painting by Anna Lee Hafer

Small, quiet room. Big, busy city.
The sun finds us anyway,
camaraderie of light in dark isolation.
We look out windows at each other.

In this way the sun finds us
brightened by the waves of strangers
as we look out windows at each other,
connected by warmth and light.

So bright these lives of strangers!
And the outside flowers brought in,
connecting us to warmth and light—
see how they cheer us!

Mornings, we bring our flowers out
to balconies, display them for each other.
See how this cheers us—
camaraderie and light amidst dark isolation.

On balconies, we display flowers for each other.
In this way, the neighborly sun finds us.
Camaraderie of light in dark isolation.
Small, quiet room. Big, busy city.

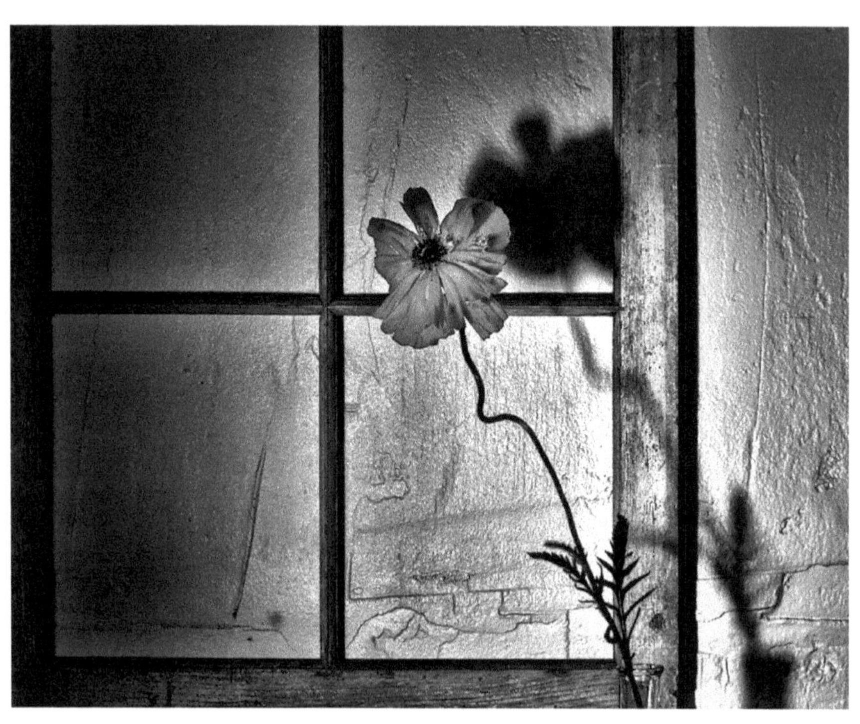

Karen Elias, *Grey Lady*, 2020

## Still Life of House Plant and Trash Can

—after the photograph *Grey Lady* by Karen Elias

Kicked outside,
withered and brittle,
we're just grey ladies,
the weather wrapping these thin limbs
in lonely and gone, in what isn't
warm enough to remember.

Remember how we sat once
by your window, warm enough
in what was: "lonely" and "gone" only
the wrappings of weather, the thin limbs
of grey-haired ladies—just strangers then,
withered and brittle, kicked outside.

# X-Ray

—after the photograph *Chiaroscuro* by Karen Elias

Like us, inside it's dying,
twig bones brittle, curled veins

worming their way toward dirt.
Or, alive—its innards

still squirming toward light—
it thrives. Like this,

one raindrop of hope
keeps all our throats open,

the thirsty need for green
so black and white,

we feel what we cannot see
there in the dank cave

of the chest or here
in the chiaroscuro of forest

where, once exposed,
each fold of flesh or leaf

strives, with heart-
shaped odds,

to emerge.

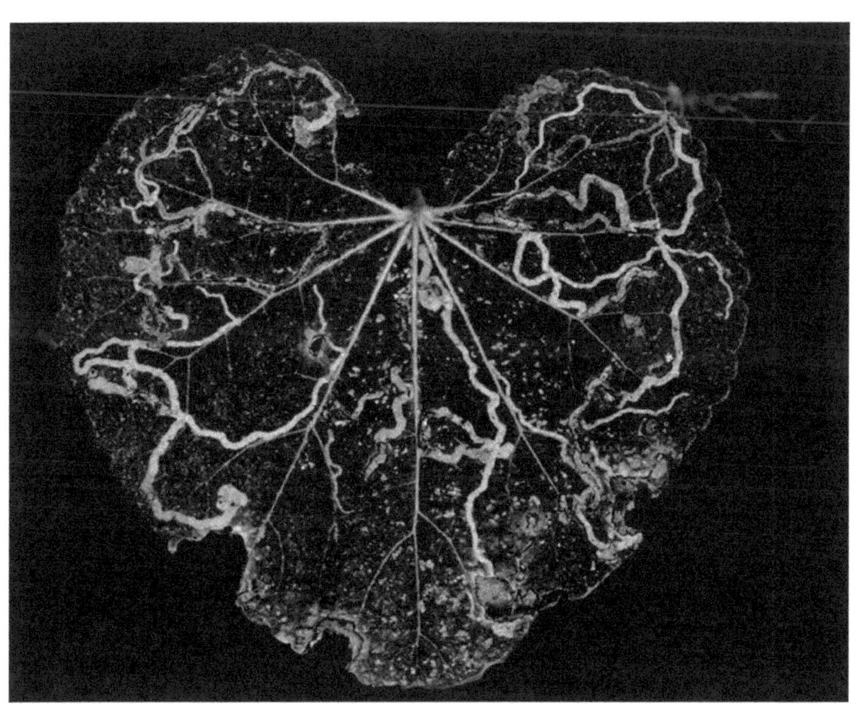

Karen Elias, *Chiaroscuro*, 2021

## At the American Visionary Art Museum: *Villa's Universe*

—artist Margaret Munz-Losch

Poster child for why
bad things happen to friends'
good daughters, she smiles slyly
while the infantile encephalitis
that nearly killed her at one hides
behind her fifteenth-century resemblance
to *Lady with an Ermine*. Necklaced beetles
& fragile butterflies, today spread wide with mercy,
clothe her. At twelve, she cradles not da Vinci's
white weasel, but her family's rescue dog
that even now rescues us who cannot explain
this universe that hurts and heals her,
punctuated just so with light, with Villa.

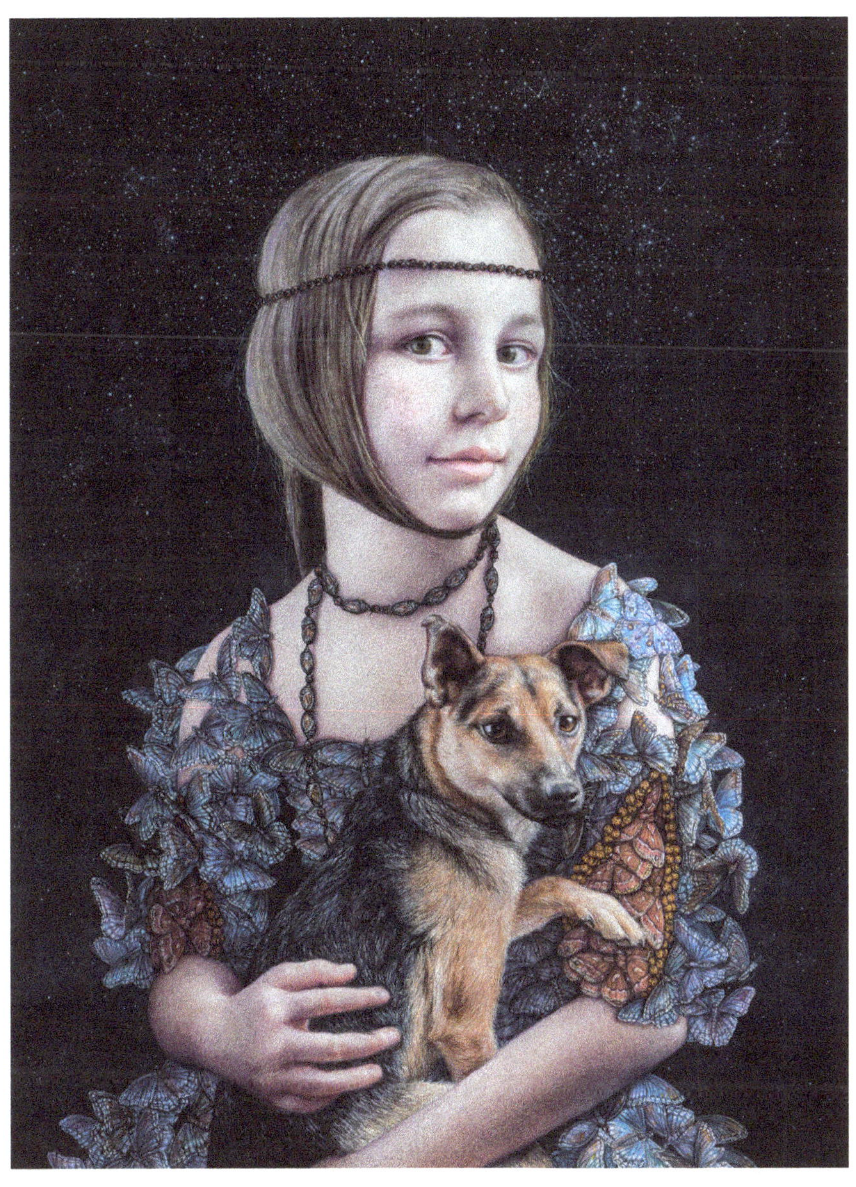

Margaret Munz-Losch, *Villa's Universe*, 2015

## At the American Visionary Art Museum: *The Watcher*

> "I think, ultimately, science and
> art ask the same question. They both
> seek a kind of beauty." —artist Greg Mort

Outside this frame,
this columned house,
this heavy door, this man,
who is us, who is standing at the threshold
not of fear of the outside but this unexpected hinged
opening to awe—ordinary suburban space that swings into Space—
splattered with the galaxy of exclamation, *yes, yes, yes,*
strange burst of forever's possibilities transporting
the artist's view to ours—us in his image—
there in his studio, here at the gallery,
but here also at the precarious brink
of stepping into the unknown,
our gaze rising to beauty,
our unsteady feet testing
first steps, with him,
into vision.

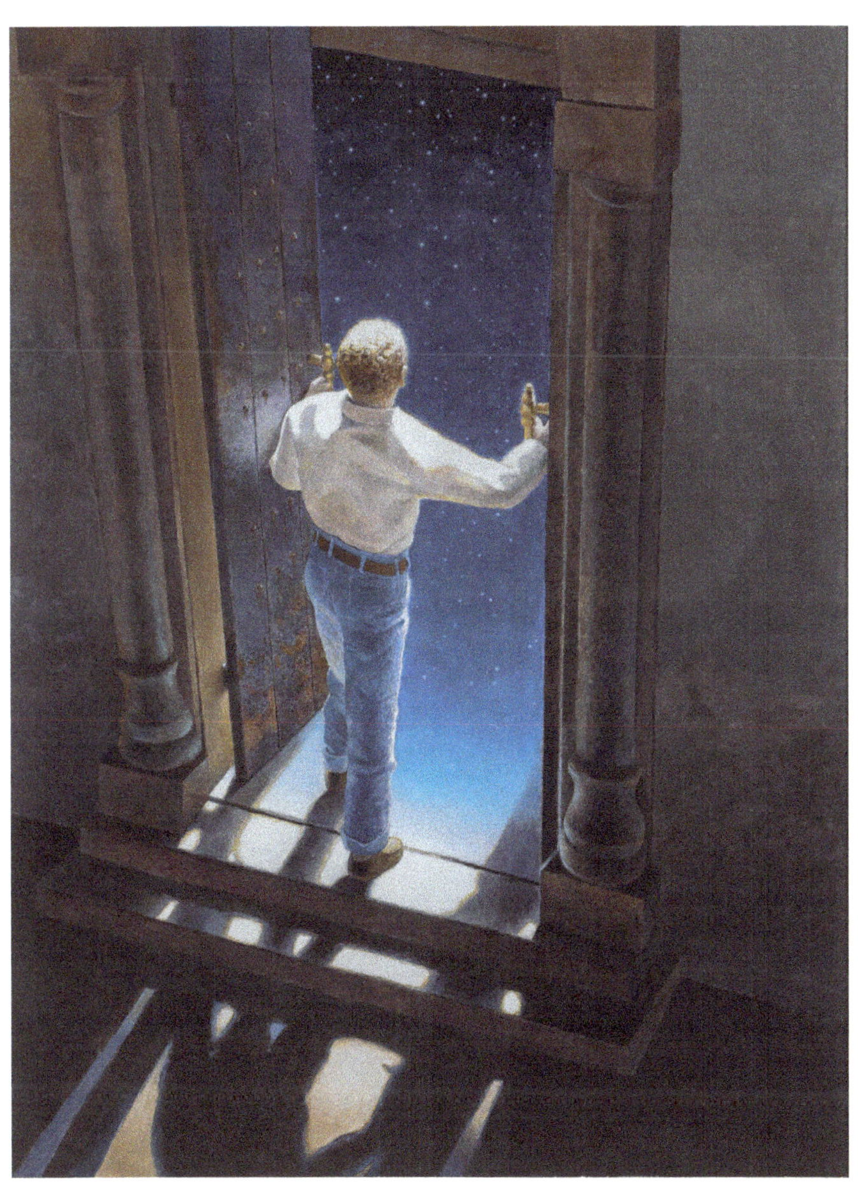

Greg Mort, *The Watcher*, 2015

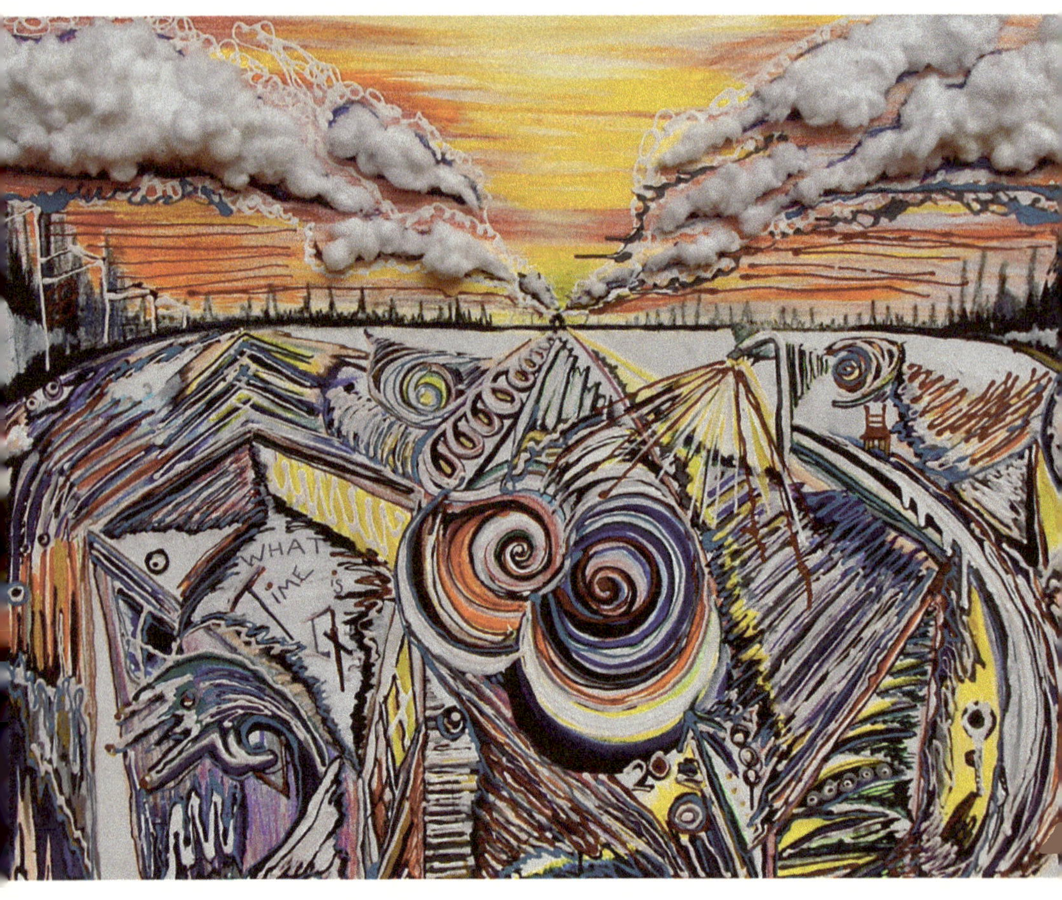


**Anna Lee Hafer, *Illegitimately Trained*, 2021**

A play on words, this title touches on society's view of the professional artist as an illegitimate career. It questions the legitimacy of the abstract style as well as representation in general, referencing similar themes initially raised by the Belgian surrealist René Magritte in his 1929 painting *Treachery of Images*. This is not a "real" train, so by default it must be illegitimate. Or does it count as "real" because it is something that still exists and is viewable? This painting questions and disputes our understanding of reality.

## Illegitimately Trained

—after the painting by Anna Lee Hafer

The cotton balls are real
and the paint. The questions are
real and the light. The small and faraway
loom as large as the not-now but-once real
yellow-orange-blue sunset or sunrise populated by
not clouds but smoke, not puffs, but cotton.
The cotton balls are real and the lines
travel someplace across landscapes
you've been to in real time or
before time or now. Never mind. The bright
lines of light shine insight, pool the eyes
with swirl that obstructs the tracks
travelled once-upon-a-time to someplace
not dream. Right? At least you'll agree,
the cotton balls are real
and the paint. The questions are
real and the light. And someone
you and not-you opened the view
to time moving while you
and not-you waited
on a small painted chair
and agreed the cotton balls are real
and the paint; the lines line-up to something
purchased at Rite-Aid and Lowe's before
the artist pulled out of an open bag,
pried out of a sealed can:
a train, the tracks,
a sky, smoke,
you. Really.
Come see.
The cotton balls are real
and the paint.

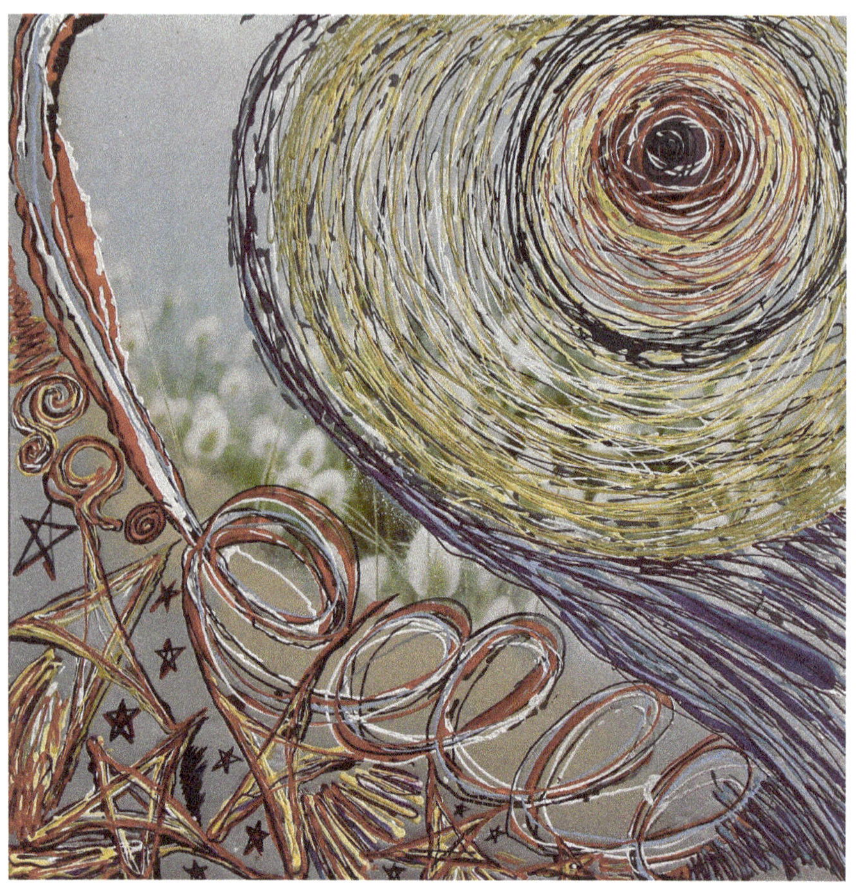

Anna Lee Hafer, *Metaphysical Vault*, 2021

A vault into day and night, land and sky, real and imaginary, this painting expands our understanding of the real world. Originally a realistic photo printed on stretched canvas, it represented the world as we knew it. Now it has become a representation of the world as the artist sees it.

# Metaphysical Vault

—after the painting by Anna Lee Hafer

Beneath this dome of sky,
breathe. Fields in spring

dial coded combinations,
shape & color clicking open

bright bursts of holy.
Beyond the ordinary

beauty of dawn and dusk,
the artist's hair-thin bristles

weave the eye's marginalia:
iris of sun, night's exclamations

doodling constellations of delight.
Ah, the awe of collage:

hands unlocking mind's focus
and filter: textured lens, layered

landscape, sight/insight of day,
paint-studded starry, starry night.

# Ante Meridiem/Post Meridiem

—after two paintings by Anna Lee Hafer

Between ante and post:
the self's permission slip

to tarry, invite the sun in
for tea and toast

spread with lazy
while the mind wanders

between in and out,
mirroring the weather

of wonder. Stay
a while

and
admire.

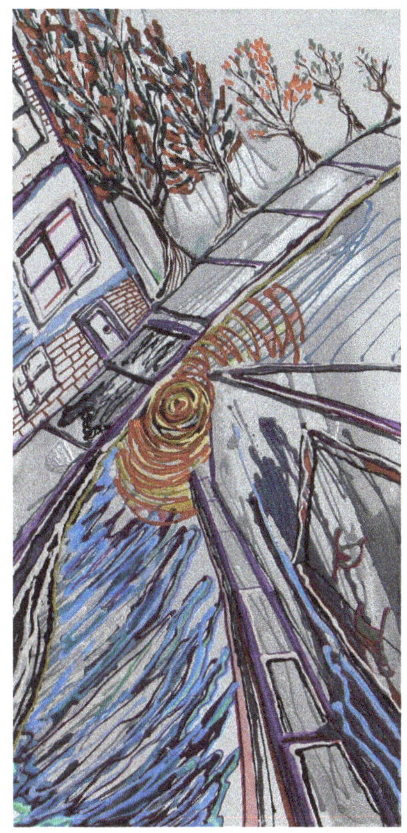

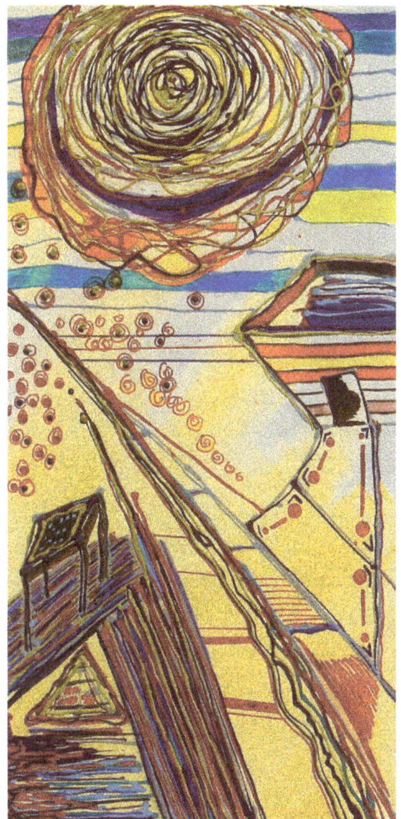

Anna Lee Hafer, *Post Meridiem* and *Ante Meridiem*, 2021

*Post Meridiem:* Evenings keep us inside our homes due to the cool temperature and lack of natural light. Here, the sun is bidding us goodbye to be reborn again in *Ante Meridiem* as a primary visual element. We face a different sense and style of isolation and admiration in both the evening and the early hours of the morning.

*Ante Meridiem:* This image captures elements of the morning and explores different ways each of us may begin our day. Many of us rush out the door to work without admiring what is around us. Here, we are forced to admire our surroundings as our breakfast table does not allow us to ignore it. Can't you feel the warmth of the sun now? Stay for a while and enjoy.

## At the American Visionary Art Museum: *Return to the Moon*

—artist Greg Mort

Imagination's always more delicious
than that sixteen-inch black-and-white
portion you watched in '69. Here
the tall pines are yours—fresh
from the backwoods of childhood—
the pock-marked, telescoped-up-close
sky—no, more like magnificent,
pungent Swiss swelling the horizon
beneath an alien's secret microscope—
the green/blue of moon-mold tempting
your conspiratorial mind with all things lunar/
lunatic, fingers ready to launch escape
to what has already landed inches away from
now, here before your ravenous eyes, still
conjuring one more flight of fancy.

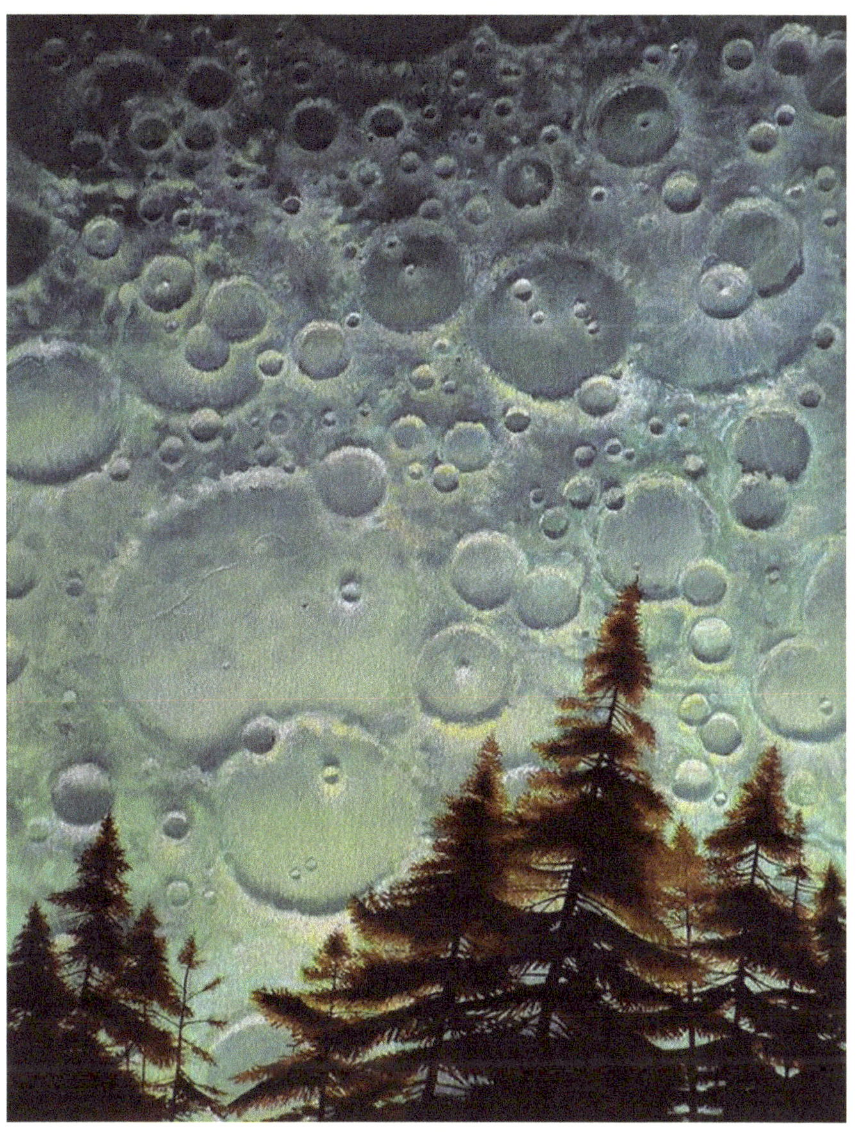

Greg Mort, *Return to the Moon*, 2009

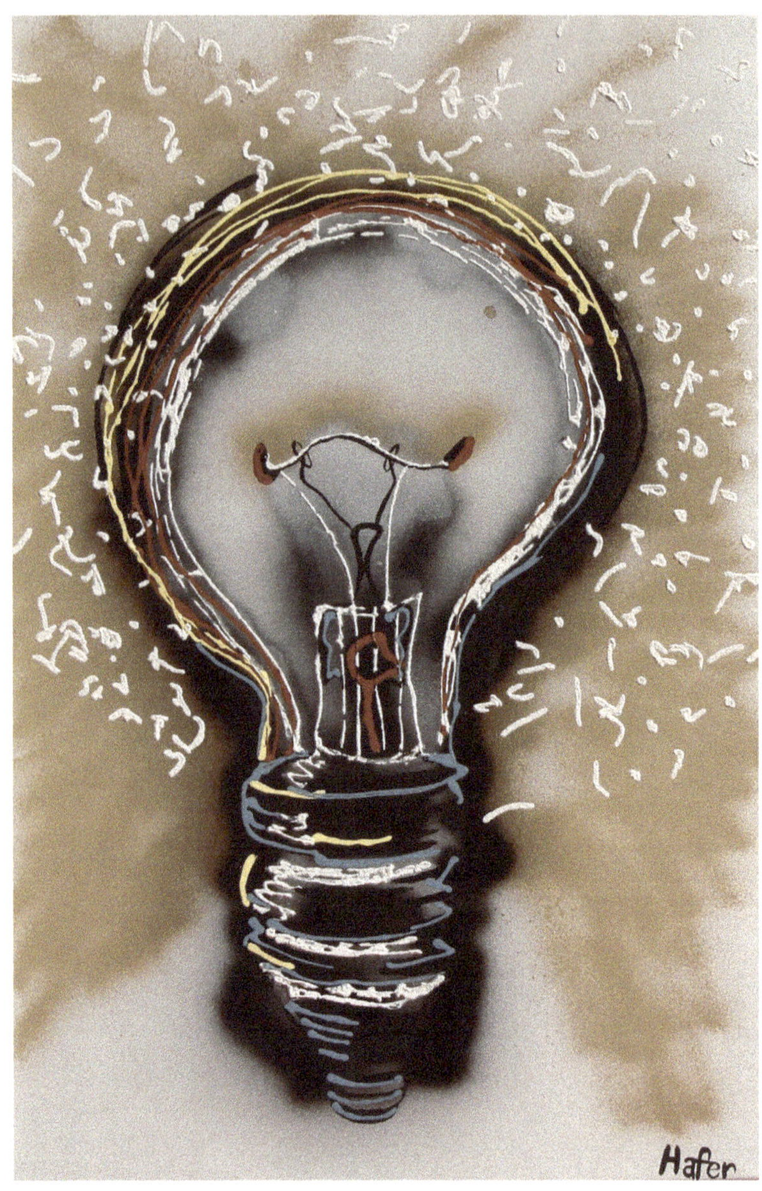


Anna Lee Hafer, *Switch*, 2021

The physical representation of a lightbulb can convey many different themes: intelligence, faith, darkness, and light.

# Switch

—after the painting by Anna Lee Hafer

Switch is a verb that lights
the brain, gets the action done.
Or a noun—off/on, dark/bright

with what it knows. Verb recites
each epiphany brilliantly. Never outdone,
Switch is a verb that lights

location, flicks on insights
to illuminate in-/exteriors. The lone
lamp of noun—on/off, dark/bright—

it shines meaning, switches day and night,
distinctions cited. It recognizes its own
and acts. Switch is a verb that lights

the foggy brain. Its decisions brighten
dim rooms with *up* not *down*.
As noun, the off/on word knows dark/bright

but waits while Verb chooses what's right.
Shrouded in shadow, Noun's tone
is passive. Switch: best as verb that lights
up noun: *off* into *on, dark* into *bright*.

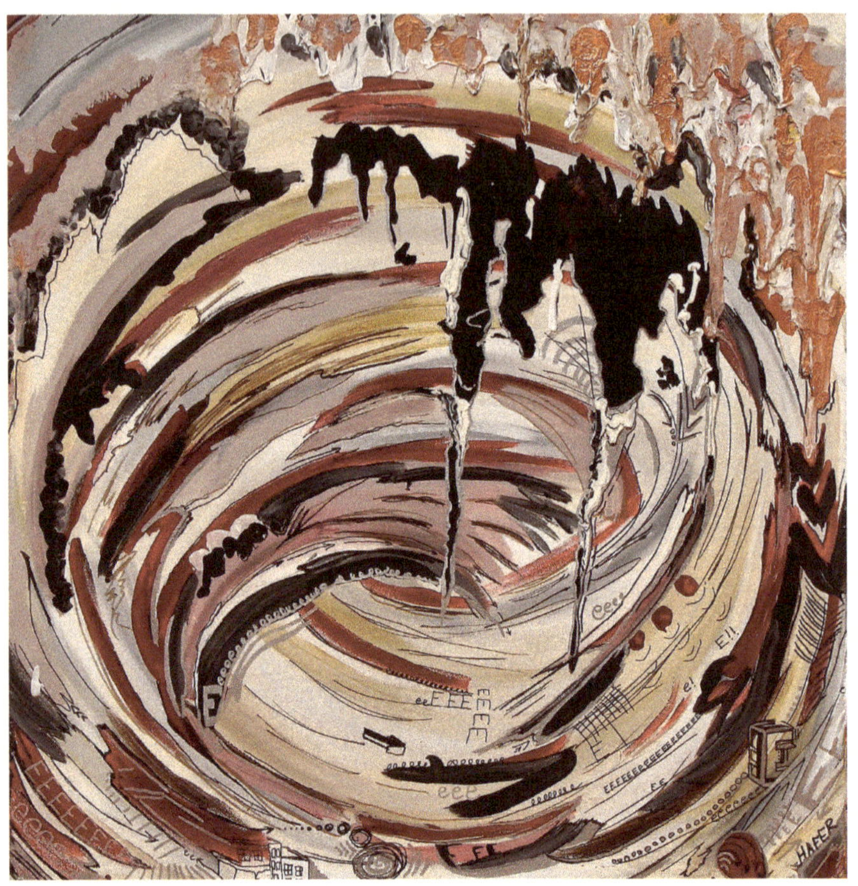


Anna Lee Hafer, *The Letter E*, 2018

*The Letter E* is a painting that questions how we absorb new information. This piece was inspired by a child penalized for asking a brilliant, creative, out-of-the-box question in class while the focus of the day was the letter E.

Does a strictly regulated and enforced schedule hurt more than help our brain's ability to absorb new information?

## The Letter E

—after the painting by Anna Lee Hafer

Don't distract me with questions,
those extraneous detours that topple learning.
E and only E is today's lesson.

The enemy of schedules is curiosity, omissions
necessary for well-paced delivery. We yearn
for no distractions. Don't ask me questions—

time-wasting, silly digressions
of how and why. Pay attention. Our concern
is E and only E. Today's lesson

is letter 5. Your inquisitive obsessions
are enemies of order. Don't ruin
class by distracting me with questions.

Creativity's the one transgression
I won't allow. Sit still. Don't squirm.
E and only E is today's lesson.

Up next? The letter F, natural progression
of learning. Quiet! It's not your turn
to talk. Don't distract me questions.
E and only E is today's lesson.

## Your Move?*

—after the painting by Anna Lee Hafer

*Why would I lie to you?* The sun glimmers like a lost
pocket watch, melting. See how it drips radiance
into each shadow/shade of thought, each mountain ravine,
each swirling field of grass arching toward evergreen?
Follow the hare wherever. Better late than never-never

falling from here to there. *Watch your step.* Inside
the mind, another landscape erupts: oversized/shrunk,
all meaning slanted. *Why would I tell you the truth?*
The missing pieces are yours for the choosing: *King or*
*pawn? Roll the dice and pick a card* to view the other side

of story. Daily, the Queen of Hearts rages.
*Why would I lie to you?* Survival is a decision
of the soul. One square forward, one square back,
one square diagonal, one square sideways. *Here?*
*There? Nowhere?* What will you make of this empty

space, the deserted chessboard filling quickly
with choice? *Time is up*. The wild sky is falling
*Why would I tell you the truth?* or rising with the flares
that you've ignited, your luminous lines and arrowed signs
leading to destinations far beyond this canvas

where the surreal whirls a vision of green that keeps
the world swaying. *Don't look up/down/here/where?*
Just breathe. *Don't look*. Just keep seeing
what's right behind the stars, the skin, the Cheshire's
grin. *Why would I lie to you? Your move*.

---

*Italicized phrases are taken from the artist's description of the work, as well as from words and phrases hidden within the painting. For a closeup of the work, go to www.hafer.work.

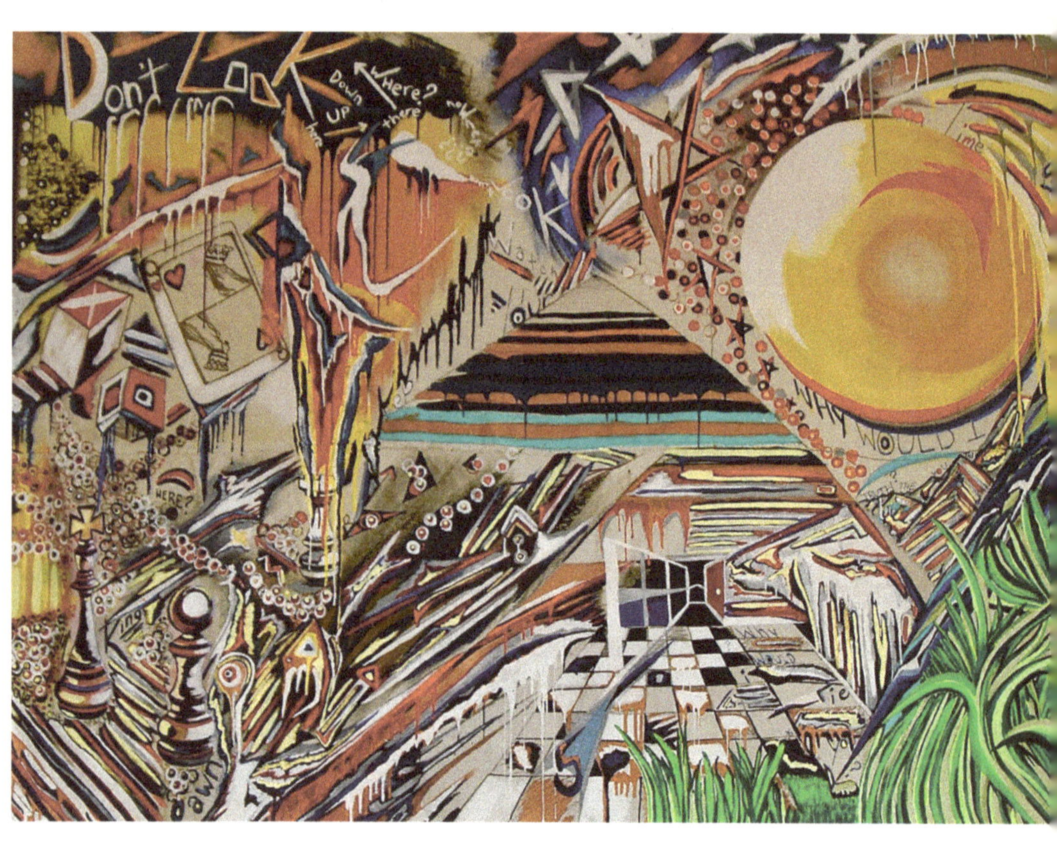


Anna Lee Hafer, *Your Move*, 2022

*Your Move* visualizes the conversation between artist and audience, in which the audience first questions the artist as a reliable and trustworthy source.

Rather than answering, the artist poses her own questions to the audience: "Why would I lie to you?" or "Why would I tell you the truth?" Each question solicits the same answer because they summarize these questions: "Why juxtapose words and diverse images without instructing the audience to 'look' ('Don't look up/down/here/there/where? . . . nowhere?' . . . 'Don't look.')?" Who is this painting really for?

Just like answers, the audience can roll the dice and pick a card. But do they follow the artist's instructions before they enter this painting of a make-believe Wonderland?

Again like questions, the artist tells her audience that it's their "move" now, before "time is up."

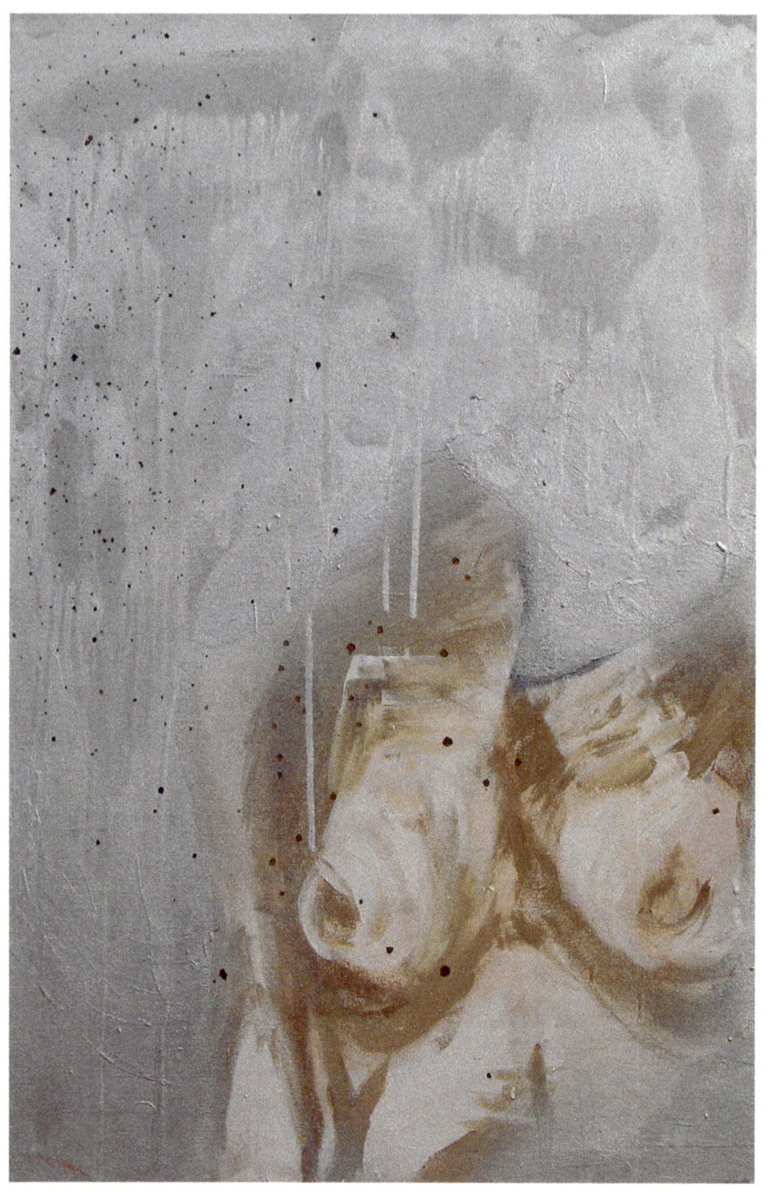

Anna Lee Hafer, *Bare Minimum*, 2018

A more minimalistic work, this painting explores the beauty of the female body without material or societal influences, bare. It also raises questions and begins an intimate conversation with the viewer on what we truly need to be happy.

## Bare Minimum

—after the painting by Anna Lee Hafer

Beneath whitewash:
sternum, neck, skull,

the fog of face,
the residue of dream

released to scream
or freedom. *No comment.*

Unclothed of skin
and woven expectations,

bone stacks on
bone, exposes the core

of caustic commentary.
What we see is

beneath the said *no comment*
is not the bared but

the unbearable *here I am*
of society's design

on us *I am*
breathing bare *here.*

## Remnants of Marjorie Maddox

—after a sculptural installation by Siobhán Arnold, mid-1990s

Disassembling "props of femininity" from the fifties—shoes,
handbags, dresses—you pull from a pink patent-leather purse

my names but not my place(s), de-construct them
these decades later with vintage store finds re-defined

as "Marjorie's": Mary Jane soles carved to sharp points;
fingernails clipped to the likeness of buttons

and arranged artfully in a velvet necklace case;
dismantled black cocktail dress and stripped lining,

through which you've projected your vision
of a rusting animal trap—all arranged on the remnants

of plush white carpet in Santa Barbara,
but also as backdrop to your grandmother:

educated career woman, mother of six in the 1950s,
caught in the sharp steel of societal expectations

at the end of that long era on the brink
of 1960s upheaval, just after

I was born half a country away in Ohio,
my name only mine, the coming wars—

both unknown and predicted—
anxious to exhibit their wares.

## At the American Visionary Art Museum: *Black Cat*

—from *Beauty and the Beast* by Margaret Munz-Losch

Startled, the bad-
omen black cat stares
at you, a voyeur suddenly here
in this stark room, uninvited,
it thinks, by the young,
pig-tailed girl whose skin
(ten shades duller than its bright
feline eyes) squirms with the intricate

pattern of maggots. Now

you cannot not see
the perched flies of eyebrows,
their green and blue bodies twitching
above her dead-sea eyes
that watch you hatching
into her, your un-combed hair
tied-up by trespass, your mind
her infested larvae of plague.

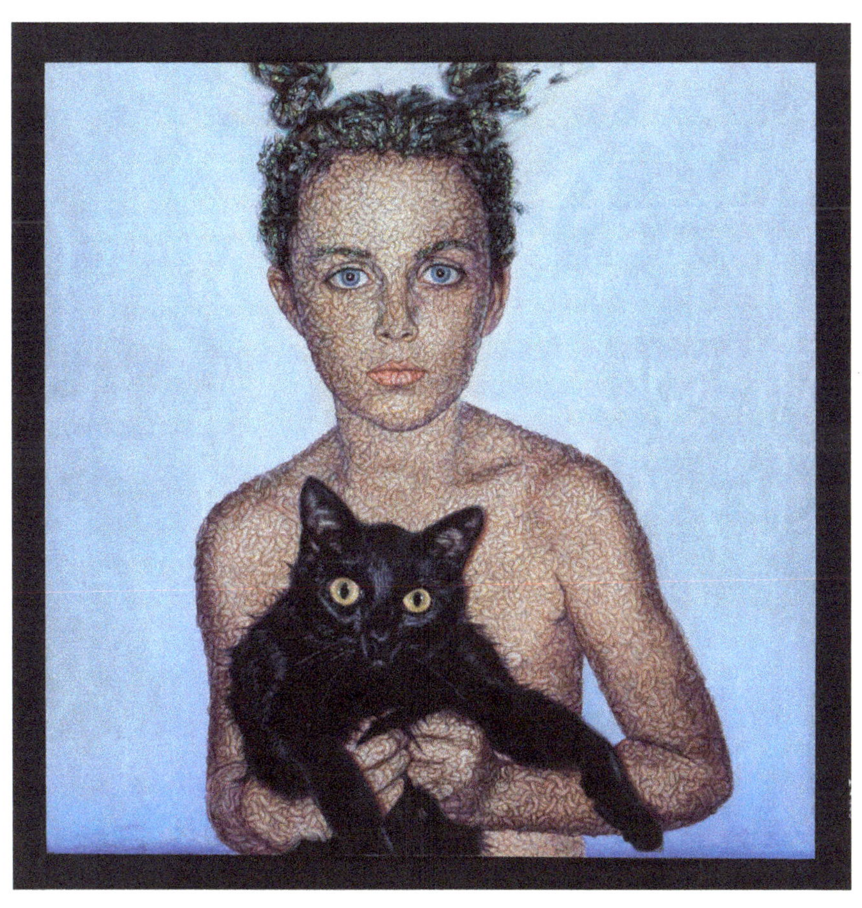

Margaret Munz-Losch, *Black Cat*, 2007

## At the American Visionary Art Museum: *Peepish Poe*

—artist Christian Twamley

Towering Master of Mystery,
mustached and tailored to the nines in vest/jacket/tie,
accompanied by obligatory cognac, ominous starry sky,
pessimistic raven, mute black cat, tell-tale heart à la carte—
all meticulously constructed with 5,000+ Easter leftovers of
    the addicted—
but first the *Why not?* out-of-the-box thinking purloined
    from the kitsch
package of marshmallow chicks into this non-horror sugar show
of nostalgia, memory the monstrosity that makes us laugh
at need, at fear, at what we do and don't want
to know of the unknown, the straightforward way
my friend's mother craved, even at death's door,
the sweet allure of Peeps, the satisfying end
of the familiar scary story.

—for Barbara Crooker

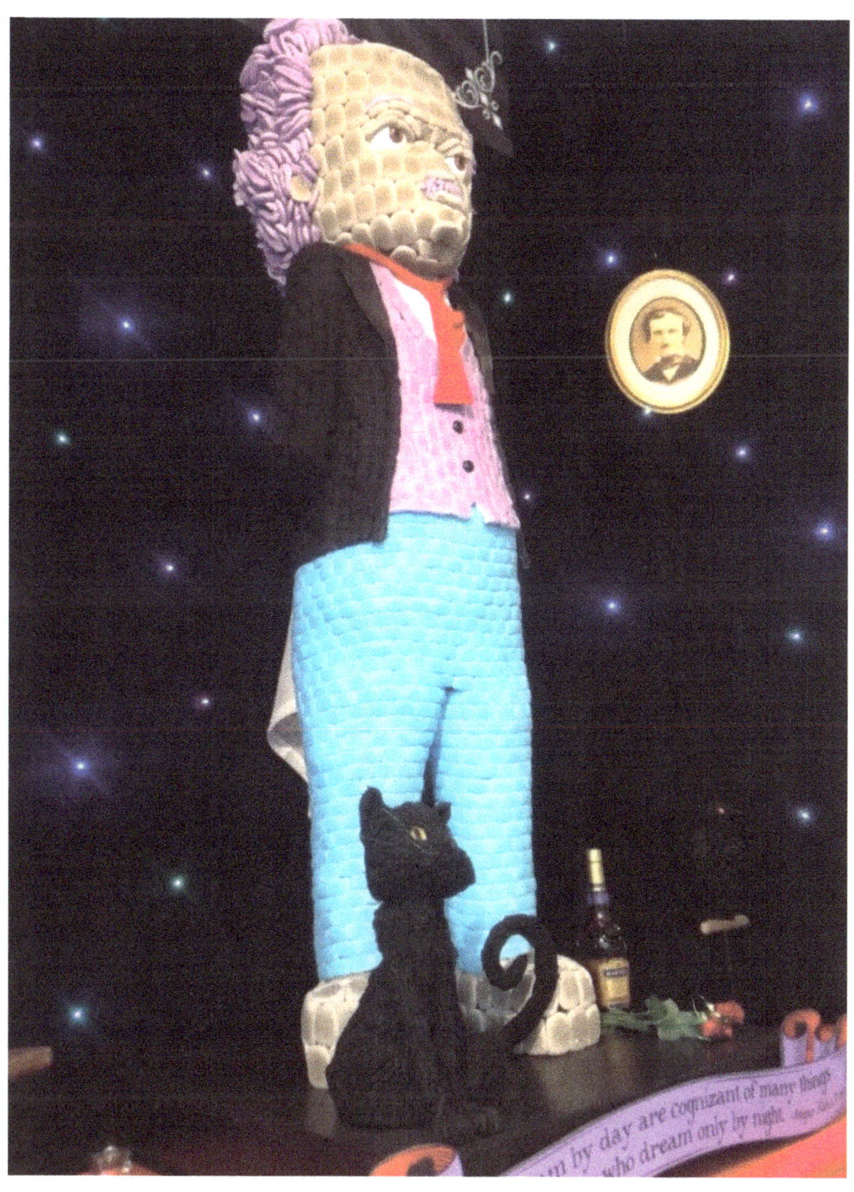


Christian Twamley, *Peepish Poe*, 2016
Photograph by Marjorie Maddox

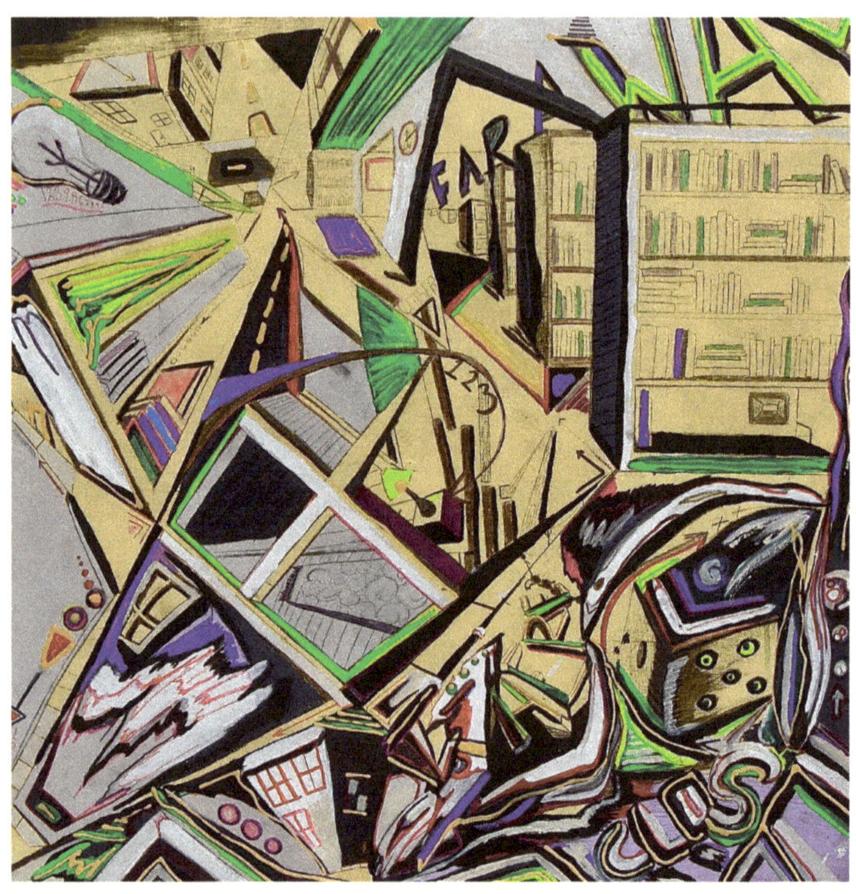

Anna Lee Hafer, *Inarticulate Archive*, 2020

This painting on wood panel explores the theme of silence. We are all aware of libraries limiting noise volume for those browsing the aisles, but did you ever consider the irony in that? Books are anything but silent. They scream to be pulled from the shelves with their enticing covers and titles. They also have an intimate and lengthy conversation between the author and reader. This archive is both quiet and loud.

# Inarticulate Archive

—after the painting by Anna Lee Hafer

"Shhh," warns the librarian
wandering between silent aisles
while, in another location,

an author types exclamations
across boisterous pages. All the while,
the librarian shushes, her warnings

ignored by long-dead historians
resurrecting theories from top shelves
while, in another location,

wig-wearing Shakespeareans
perform elaborate dress rehearsals
warning the shushed librarian

to lighten up or face eviction
from overpopulated rows of novelists
who, in another location, chant,

"Close. Faraway. Setting! Setting! Setting!"
before banning all quiet archives
of librarians, their inarticulate warnings.
    Meanwhile, in other locations. . .

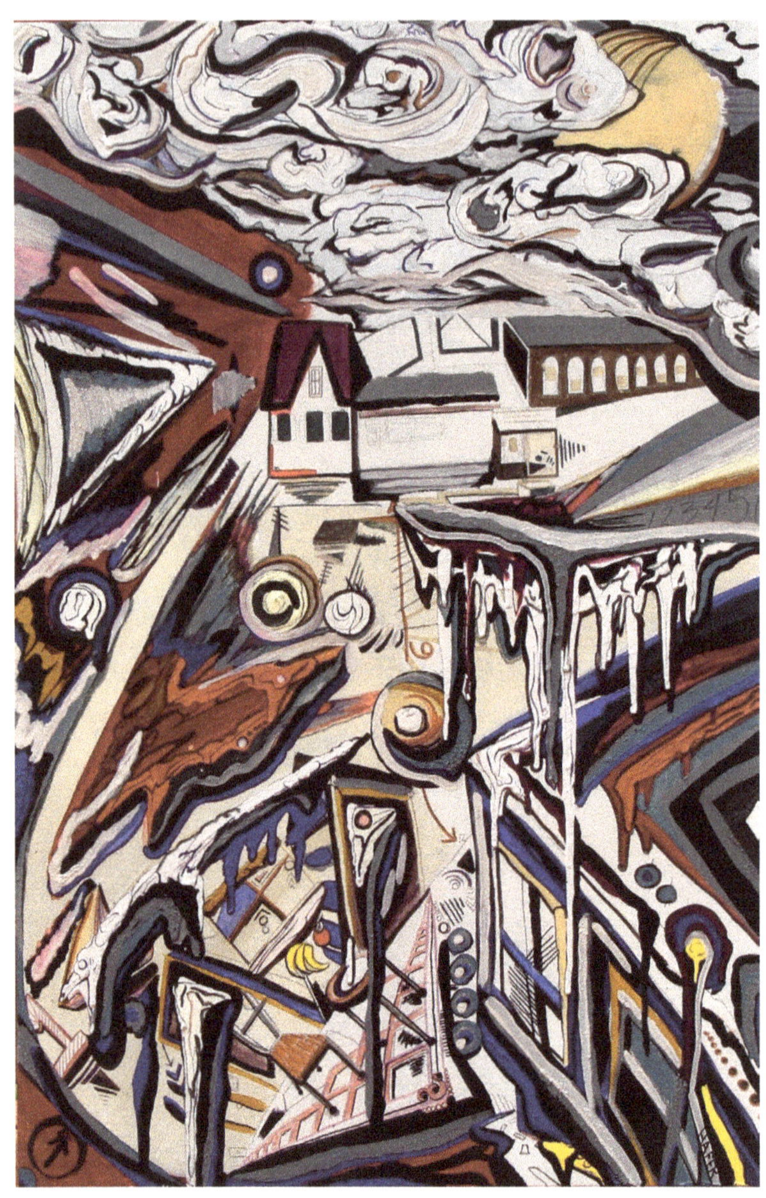

Anna Lee Hafer, *King Street*, 2020

*King Street* displays a distorted view from the artist's studio, a combination of interior and exterior spaces.

## King Street

—after the painting by Anna Lee Hafer

In/out, up/down any city/
town tacked to the frame

of a window with someone
not you looking out/

looking in. What is the point
of point of view?

The apple on the tree
or the counter? The apple

of my eye slicing the view
into juicy sections

while the downtown tilts
this way or that and the who

who sees it all devours
or nibbles between lines

that could be sun or paint
or poem or street

or icicle melting,
or mind meandering

here or there, now
or now.

# At the American Visionary Art Museum: *Madre Dolorosa*

—artist Ingo Swann

O invocator of auras, practitioner
of the remote view, of gender fluidity,

dressed as a nun at Studio 45, you
nevertheless adore her, Mother of Sorrows;

claim as yours her consciousness; then
weep with her on this canvas for a world

where sacred and cosmic comingle/
collide, phallic-like comets

spiraling toward South America,
atomic mushrooms erupting

from an ocean of tears below
the sacred temple of her heart.

Lavender and rose, you rise
in this specter of paint and space

to bow down to apparition,
*Mother Mary, pray for us*

to complexity, even to the ecstasy
of grief *now and at the hour*

at the hour of her contemplation,
*of our deaths* at thc hour of your creation,

*Madre Dolorosa* at the hour
of your invocation of this

doomsday vision.
*Amen*. Amen.

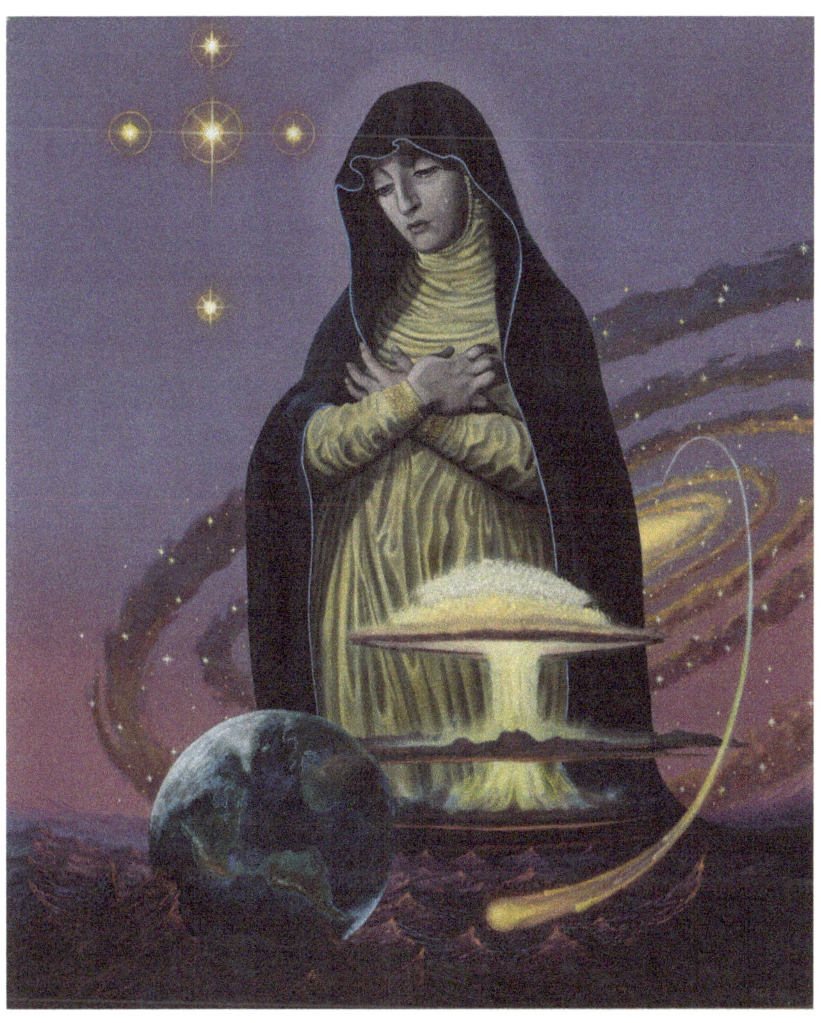

Ingo Swann, *Madre Dolorosa*, 1986
Photograph by Dan Meyers

# Two Poems after Two Photographs by Karen Elias

*Ligularia*

Hungry,
this "little tongue"
now licks the sky flipped
to ominous, our opposite
of sun.

The sun
so ominous, the opposite
of now. Flip and the sky licks
this "little tongue,"
hungry.

*Inversion*

Ligularia, stingray on a stem,
you coast just below the eye
of our storm, white underbelly
tipped toward a battered sky.
By your side, that other one is
ready to unfurl its tight
sail of change, inverting
everything.

Everything
inverts with change, sail
ready to unfurl, tight
fists by our side, now open. We are the other
tipped. Unbatter the sky
with its after-storm, underbelly of white,
coast of shore we eye as hope. Below
the stingrays: waves of bloom—ligularia.

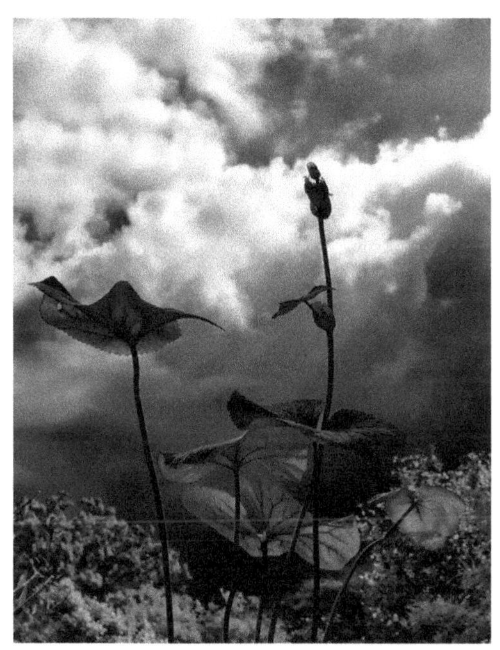

Karen Elias, *Ligularia in Black and White*, 2013

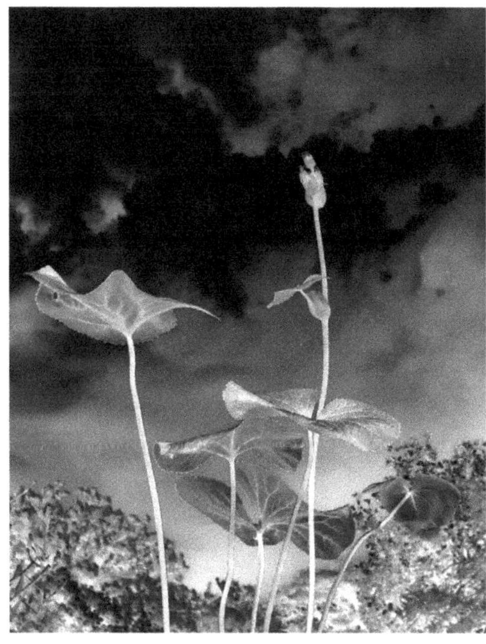

Karen Elias, *Inverted Ligularia*, 2013

## Ark

—after the painting by Anna Lee Hafer

Ladders to below/above to
turn off the faucet to

weeping to
turn on the spigot to

here/now to
unleash the liquid to

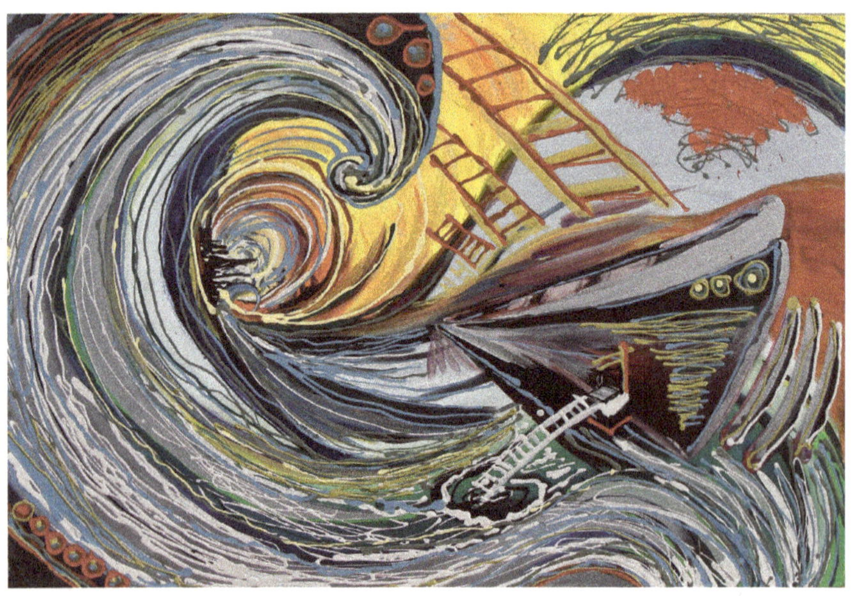

Anna Lee Hafer, *Ark*, 2021

*Ark* is an apocalypse with tsunami-like waves crashing and rolling milliseconds from the end of it all. *Ark* is a new beginning, a journey with a purpose, a safe haven completely your own.

water to weary to whiplash to
swirl in the iris of horizon to

witness the wet of windswept to
hide in the eye of reject to

float in the drowning of hopeless to
breathe in the rattling of broken to

gasp with the mouth of ocean to
curl with the swish of sudden to

gulp with the whir of twisters to
swallow with the salt of senseless to

blur with the vision of serpents to
spew with the sputum of whales to

reek with the regurgitation of Jonah to
sink in the rise of remorse to

know with the blind-eye of Noah to
soar on the dry-sky with dove to

circle the submersion of world to
flutter and hover to

dive and discover to
finally land.

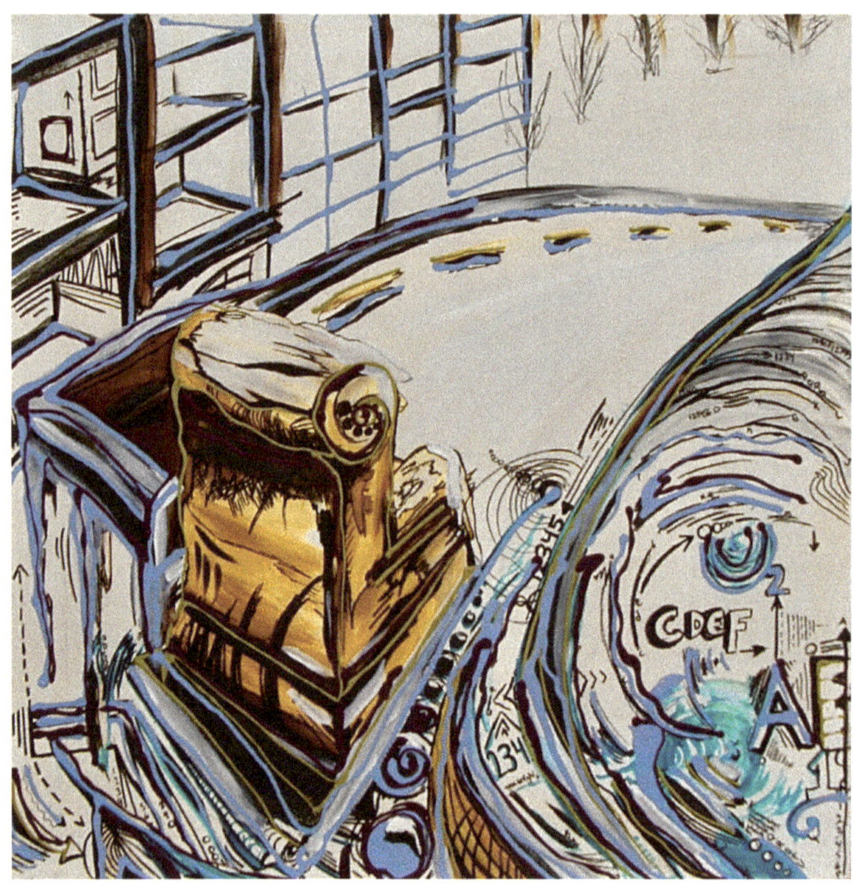


Anna Lee Hafer, *Wild Rest*, 2021

What does it mean to rest? It's something that seems simple; yet in today's society, it is something many of us must relearn. Only when we are alone do our minds reach their true potential.

## Wild Rest

—after the painting by Anna Lee Hafer

What does it mean to rest
this lazy afternoon in an overstuffed chair,
gazing out at a world so wild
with wonder the mind cannot help but wander
out amidst the trees, relax
in the hammock of wind?

In this cushioned space, imagination rewinds
the mind with quiet, calls in the calm. The rest
of the house yawns, while you stretch out, relax
into the imprint of self in the tattered chair
before the familiar view—a wonder
really, the paradox of renewal, its wild

witness of a world gone wild
with vision, passive breeze become wind
whipping into adventure to wander
the rugged terrain of contemplation. Likewise, rest
is a carnival tour of the spontaneous. Strap in. This chair's
rollercoaster ride begins with relaxation

while the brain unbuckles boundaries. Relax
and the mind climbs high. Breathe and, far below, wild
Whack-a-Moles pop in and out of fields. From a simple chair,
well worn with inspiration, the valley's wind
carries you both to and beyond the now. The rest
is the miracle of repose, the way doze leads to wander

*and* wonder, fun house of mind's museum. Wander
the labyrinth of spirit. Inhale, exhale, relax,
breathing in the scent of the Divine each blessed rest
of Sabbath. Creation's electric chariot ride to the wild
begins with *Be still and know*, all paths wind-
ing back to this room and its well-worn chair.

So, count to 10. Sing childhood's ABCs in the same chair
where your mother rocked you into a world of wonder,
where you first learned that breath and wind
are cousins reciting rituals of relaxation
in a world steeped in chaos. Embrace the wild
in calm, the journey in rest.

Here, in this chair: the origins of wander.
Here, the rhythm of wind breathing relaxation,
daily recreated in your own wild, wild rest.

## Author and Artists

Professor of English and Creative Writing at Lock Haven University of Pennsylvania, **Marjorie Maddox** has published fourteen collections of poetry—including *Transplant, Transport, Transubstantiation* (Yellowglen Prize), *True, False, None of the Above* (2017 Illumination Book Award Medalist), *Local News from Someplace Else, Perpendicular As I* (Sandstone Book Award), *Begin with a Question* (Winner Poetry/Religious Category 2022 International Book Awards), and *Heart Speaks, Is Spoken For* (Shanti Arts), an ekphrastic collaboration with photographer Karen Elias. In addition, she has published the short story collection *What She Was Saying* and four children's and YA books—including *Inside Out: Poems on Writing and Reading Poems with Insider Exercises* (Finalist Children's Educational Category 2020 International Book Awards), *A Crossing of Zebras: Animal Packs in Poetry,* and *I'm Feeling Blue, Too!* (a 2021 NCTE Notable Poetry Book)—as well as the anthologies *Common Wealth: Contemporary Poets on Pennsylvania* and the forthcoming *Keystone: Contemporary Poets on Pennsylvania* (co-editor with Jerry Wemple, PSU Press). The assistant editor of *Presence: A Journal of Catholic Poetry,* she is the recipient of numerous awards and gives workshops and readings around the world. For more information, please visit www.marjoriemaddox.com.

**Anna Lee Hafer** is a studio artist in the Philadelphia area who graduated from Roberts Wesleyan College, Rochester, New York, in 2019. Her art includes studio exhibitions at Davison Art Gallery and Rochester

Contemporary Art Center in Rochester, New York, as well as published images or broadsides in *Still Point Arts Quarterly, The Westchester Review, The Penn Review, The Pine Cone Review, Open: Journal of Arts & Letters, The Ekphrastic Review*, and elsewhere. Her work is heavily influenced by such surrealist painters as René Magritte, Salvador Dali, and Pablo Picasso, all of whom strove to build their own realities through small glimpses into a particularly confusing, but utterly unique, worldview that dictates its own specific set of instructions. In her work, Hafer pours and layers paint to create dimension and texture, mixing different styles and colors onto each other until they produce a 3D effect. Through marker and pencil that create shadow, she further enhances these forms and separates them from the background. Heavier layers and thicker brushes in the foreground of her work push the painting toward the viewer, whereas the thinner layers and small brushes in the background elongate the space and push away from the viewer. By juxtaposing interior and exterior elements, Hafer makes the audience question whether they are looking at something inside or outside. For additional information, please visit www.hafer.work.

## Contributing Artists

Karen Elias
https://www.escapeintolife.com/collaboration/collaboration-marjorie-maddox-and-karen-elias

Antar Mikosz
https://visionary.art/author/antar-mikosz

Greg Mort
https://www.gregmortcollection.com

Margaret Munz-Losch
https://www.margaretmunzlosch.com

Ingo Swann
https://ingoswann.com

Christian Twamley
https://www.mutualart.com/Artist/Christian-Twamley/9BF3F8D3D8220F83/Biography

## Supporting Organizations

The American Visionary Art Museum
https://www.avam.org

Lock Haven University of Pennsylvania
http://lockhaven.edu

# SHANTI ARTS

NATURE ▪ ART ▪ SPIRIT

Please visit us online
to browse our entire book catalog,
including poetry collections and fiction,
books on travel, nature, healing, art,
photography, and more.

Also take a look at our highly regarded art
and literary journal, *Still Point Arts Quarterly*,
which may be downloaded for free.

www.shantiarts.com

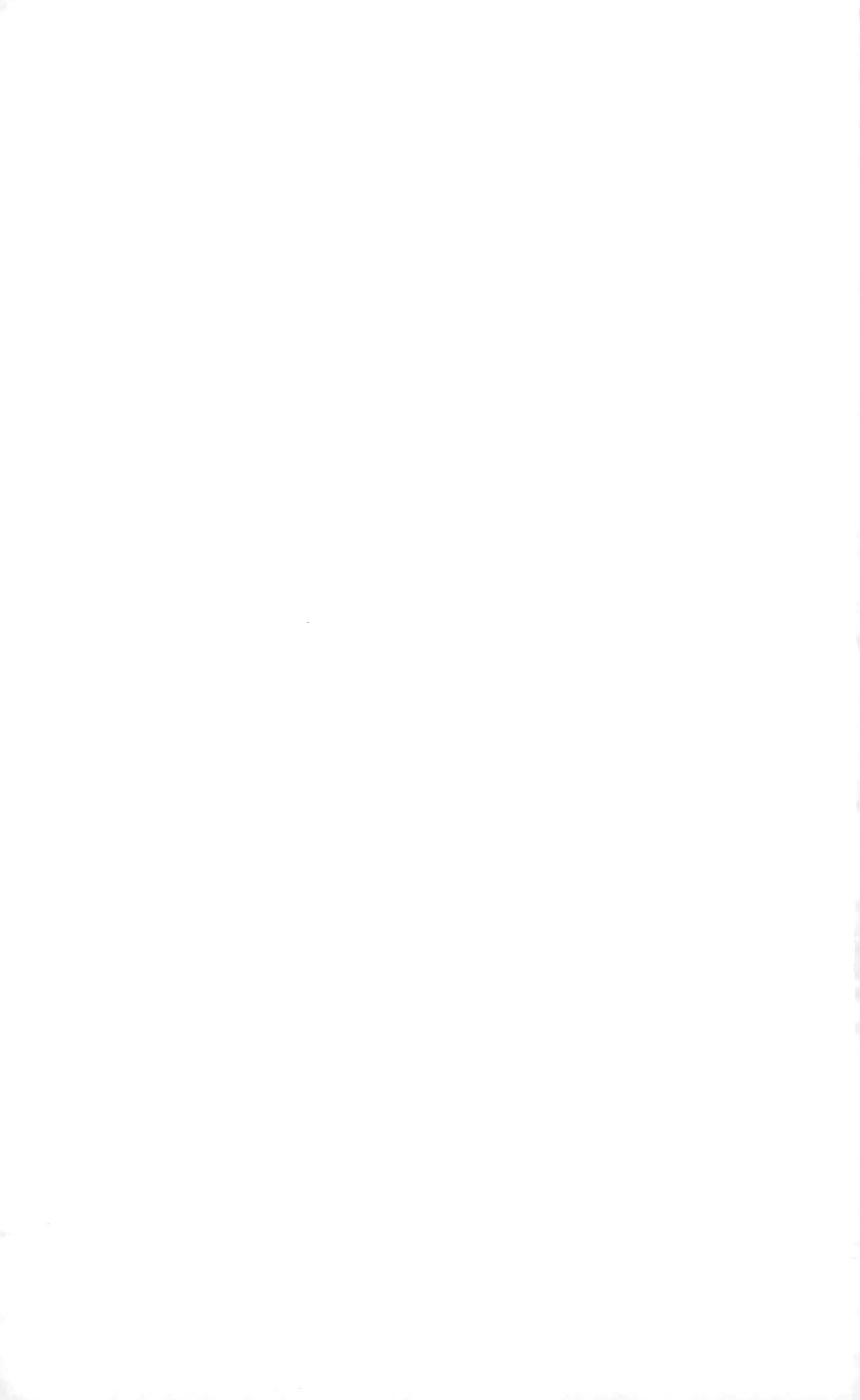

www.ingramcontent.com/pod-product-compliance
Lightning Source LLC
LaVergne TN
LVHW052355100826
845147LV00013B/847

* 9 7 8 1 9 5 6 0 5 6 7 4 7 *